PROJECT MANAGING E-LEARNING

Bill Shackelford

ASTD Press

ASTD Press is an internationally renowned source of insightful and practical information on workplace learning and performance topics, including training basics, evaluation and return-on-investment (ROI), instructional systems development (ISD), e-learning, leadership, and career development.

Ordering information: Books published by ASTD Press can be purchased by visiting our Website at store.astd.org or by calling 800.628.2783 or 703.683.8100.

Library of Congress Control Number: 2002104901

ISBN-10: 1-56286-329-0
ISBN-13: 978-1-56286-329-6

Printed by Victor Graphics, Inc., Baltimore, MD.
www.victorgraphics.com

Contents

Preface

Ten years from now the term *e-learning* will probably sound as quaint and redundant as "computerization" or "office automation." I'll bet that in the last half of the 15th century there were conferences, workshops, and seminars on "MT-Learning," touting the virtues of movable type to bring knowledge to the masses, hawking new printing technologies, and creating vast new industries for scholars and artisans. Those medieval marketing folks were at least halfway right: Movable type changed everything. It made book production cheaper so that more people could access the written word, it set the stage for the global distribution of knowledge, it opened new markets for writers, and it created a whole new print-based industry that continues to thrive in today's digital world.

Today, we take movable type for granted, and in a short while we'll do the same thing with e-learning. But, for right now, the e-learning revolution is real and forces all learning professionals to think in new ways about how and where people learn. It also means revisiting some well-established principles of course development, technology deployment, and project management to deliver e-learning. This book will help get you started.

WHO SHOULD READ THIS BOOK?

ASTD's e-learning series is a body of knowledge and tools for all who are interested in initiating or improving e-learning within their organizations. This book focuses on how to define, plan, manage, and review an e-learning project. Four main types of audiences can benefit from this book:

1. *Course developers:* Usually course developers have a solid grasp of how people learn, how to establish learning objectives, and how to assemble and deliver learning content in a classroom setting. Whether they realize it or not, they have demonstrated project management skills as well. This book introduces formal project management principles to help them

develop reproducible processes for delivering courses in the e-learning environment.

2. *Traditional project managers:* Although most of the project management principles outlined here will be familiar to project managers, their application to online learning environments offers some new challenges. The processes and sample forms in this book provide some suggestions for establishing an e-learning project methodology that can evolve as the organization implements and expands its e-learning initiatives.

3. *Information technology (IT) staff and Web designers:* The IT department often is the last to get involved in e-learning initiatives, but the staff of this department will be critical members of the team involved in creating and supporting e-learning content. The sooner the IT department is involved, the less likely course developers are to select incompatible technologies or harbor unrealistic expectations about what's required to support and maintain e-learning from a technical standpoint. Web designers need to understand the importance of reusability and standardization in setting up a viable e-learning environment. Both groups should become familiar with the aims of e-learning and the methods used for delivering e-learning. Web designers and IT staff may already be familiar with some of the project management techniques outlined here, including the concept of delivery cycles and a focus group approach (or at least the idea of using joint application design/development). This book can give both groups a better overview of the e-learning delivery process so that they can take a proactive role in delivering high-quality e-learning within their organizations.

4. *E-learning project sponsors:* Admittedly, some of this book provides greater detail than project sponsors or senior managers need to stay informed about e-learning projects. Nevertheless, project sponsors and others responsible for promoting or assessing the value of e-learning within the organization need insights into the e-learning delivery process, and they need to know what their roles should be in that process. If you are in this group of readers, feel free to skip the gory details of project estimation and concentrate on some of the "big picture" areas such as risk and change management, the overall incremental delivery approach, and how e-learning project managers should handle progress and problem reporting.

WHAT'S UNIQUE ABOUT THIS BOOK?

The book is designed to help you formulate a strategy for delivering e-learning products based on traditional project management principles and, at the same time, reflects some of the latest thinking about delivering applications for business and for the Web.

Part 1 serves as an introduction to the principles of project management. Here you'll find essential background materials for defining, planning, managing, and reviewing e-learning projects. Part 2 covers the steps in getting an e-learning project under way and provides a framework for classifying various types of e-learning projects—from huge total e-curriculum development projects down to miniprojects for producing specific e-learning components. Part 3 takes you through an iterative e-learning project and illustrates the process of planning and managing delivery cycles so that your customers stay involved throughout the project. In addition, this section provides techniques for evaluating each project to help create an environment of continuous improvement when delivering e-learning products in the future.

Each chapter ends with a "Your Turn" section designed to help you apply the ideas presented to your own situation. The worksheets provided in these sections are also available on the book's companion Website: www.projectmanagingelearning.com, so you do not have to write on the worksheets provided in this book.

ACKNOWLEDGMENTS

I owe much of this book to some key influences in my thinking about project management and to a number of others who provided encouragement and suggestions as the book progressed. First of all, I want to thank Lou Russell, chief executive officer of Russell Martin & Associates, who has been a mentor and colleague throughout the past decade. Second, many of the concepts about iterative cyclical delivery of projects come from Jim Highsmith, whose groundbreaking book *Adaptive Software Development* showed how to create software products using iterative cycles and collaborative teams with close customer involvement. E-learning projects are natural candidates for this kind of approach, and my book shows how to apply it. I especially want to thank Jon Aleckson, chief executive officer of Web Courseworks, whose encouragement, real-world e-learning project management templates, and experienced advice proved invaluable as I created what I hope will be a truly practical guide to managing e-learning projects.

Finally, several friends and spiritual mentors have provided invaluable support. I thank Joette Waters, Marsha Haake, Sally Maro, Wendy Smith, Pam Hager, and John Sears. They all believed in me more than I believed in myself. I'm a very lucky author.

Bill Shackelford

Part 1
Basic Principles
of Project Management

The six chapters in this section cover the principles and practices of project management and provide pointers on how to achieve success in delivering e-learning projects on time and within budget. If you are already an experienced project manager, some of this material will be familiar to you. If you are already producing e-learning content, you will also find yourself revisiting basic e-learning concepts.

You may just skim chapters that cover familiar territory, but along the way look for some new insights into how e-learning projects differ from most course development projects. If you've already successfully created e-learning courses, you may very likely discover some project management tips and techniques to make the next e-learning project an even greater success.

1

Putting Discipline Into the Management of E-Learning Projects

If you have taken on the job of managing your organization's e-learning initiative, it's probably because you have already proven yourself to be an effective learning specialist with a record of completing assignments on time and within budget. The rapid growth of e-learning and the increasing demand to deliver quality learning environments quickly raises the bar for course developers and project managers. You will need new project management approaches and new methods of delivery. You'll need creative new ways to deliver e-learning experiences that meet the needs of learners and their managers. This chapter reveals what's different about e-learning projects. Subsequent chapters revisit traditional project management principles and show how they apply to e-learning.

WHY E-LEARNING?

William Horton's straightforward definition of e-learning says it all: "E-learning is the use of Web and Internet technologies to create experiences that educate our fellow human beings" (Horton, 2001a). Notice the broad scope of this definition, especially if you originally thought that e-learning only referred to educating the employees within your organization. Your first e-learning ventures may very well target an internal audience, but don't be surprised if you're soon in the business of educating business partners, suppliers, and customers through e-learning!

Like the Web itself, the potential for e-learning is practically unlimited, gaining momentum as more people become e-learners and begin to expect and demand engaging, Web-enabled interactive learning experiences.

UP UNTIL NOW

Until recently, e-learning was most likely a secondary endeavor in the training programs for organizations. The greatest headway had been in training in technical skills or in areas where much detailed information needed to be transferred via rote learning. Many corporate trainers were skeptical that e-learning could be an effective tool for teaching "soft skills" or that Web-based experiences could ever match the interaction achievable in a classroom environment.

The word is out now that well-designed e-learning courses can provide similar or better learning experiences than what is usually available in the classroom. Reasons for this include the following:

- Course developers and designers are beginning to create powerful, engaging interactive e-learning experiences rather than merely transferring classroom textual materials to the Web.
- Course modules are available to the learner when the learner needs the material rather than according to a fixed class schedule.
- E-learning courses can make available the knowledge of world-renowned experts.
- E-learning materials are easier to keep up-to-date than traditional classroom materials are.
- It's as easy to provide e-learning to hundreds of learners as it is to a few.

E-Learning Environments

E-learning has expanded beyond the college and university and corporate environments, where it evolved out of computer-based training, to embrace virtually every individual on the Internet. As the availability of e-learning continues to expand, those responsible for e-learning development will need to coordinate their individual course development projects with a burgeoning array of competing and complementary course offerings.

It will become increasingly necessary to make "build versus buy" decisions for providing e-learning. And, you will constantly need to redefine your e-learning audience. Corporations will certainly need to introduce e-learning experiences to build and maintain the skill levels of their employees; and schools, colleges, and universities will continue to expand their Web-based course offerings. At the same time, more and more organizations will introduce value chain e-learning (sometimes called "educommerce") to educate partners, suppliers, distributors, resellers, and customers to remain competitive.

Goals of E-Learning

E-learning tries to address the growing need for just-in-time learning, to provide performance support to a widely dispersed workforce, to accommodate rapidly changing course content, and to leverage course development costs

Why E-Learning Projects Fail

You, as project manager, can keep your e-learning projects on track by avoiding a few common pitfalls. If you keep these in mind when creating and implementing your e-learning project plans, your e-learning projects stand a greater chance for success. So, without further ado, here are the top 18 reasons e-learning projects fail (drum roll, please):

18. failure to set forth an e-learning strategy that takes into account the most pressing business needs of your organization
17. failure to create an organizational context with clearly delineated roles and responsibilities for the e-learning development team and the other stakeholders in the e-learning project
16. failure to recognize that e-learning, like most other Web-based initiatives, requires adaptive, incremental processes
15. failure to perform meaningful reviews of e-learning development at the end of each project to ensure continuous process improvement for subsequent e-learning projects
14. failure to view e-learning modules as dynamic entities that will require ongoing maintenance to stay current
13. failure to manage risks, take precautions to mitigate threats to the proj-ect, and invest the time and effort necessary to develop contingency plans
12. creation of e-learning courses that merely imitate (often poorly) traditional classroom offerings
11. failure to distinguish between technology dazzle and real learning value
10. failure to build modularity and reusability into e-learning courses
9. lack of a change management strategy
8. failure to keep all customers and stakeholders involved and aligned with the e-learning goals of the organization
7. failure to dedicate full-time support to the e-learning initiative
6. failure of the information technology department to provide technical and funding support
5. failure to plan for the physical architecture required to support e-learning
4. failure to recognize the magnitude of the technological component
3. failure to document projects and to share documents within the project and with other e-learning projects within the organization
2. being "held hostage" by multimedia stars who so completely dominate the project that schedules slip and standardization is not possible.

And, the number one reason for e-learning project failure is:

1. lack of ongoing support from management.

Guess what? A lack of management support is the single most commonly cited reason for almost *all* project failures! Your role as project manager demands that you cultivate champions who will sponsor your project, that you maintain their commitment through successful incremental delivery of useful e-learning content, that you manage expectations, and that you make it clear that e-learning requires continuing support.

through savings in travel costs and the ability to disperse learning content to many participants within a narrow timeframe. E-learning can do all this and more, but its very success sometimes can doom it to failure.

THE "WATERFALL PROJECT" PHILOSOPHY

Traditionally, project management has followed a "waterfall" approach. This approach uses a sequence of phases:

- definition and approval of a set of requirements
- creation of a timeline and budget to produce the deliverables defined in the requirements phase
- a design and implementation phase to produce the deliverables
- a postmortem to evaluate success and failure in producing the deliverables on time and within budget.

Because no phase is revisited once completed (hence the term *waterfall*), the most critical phase is often the requirements phase. Once the requirements are defined, any change to them is often treated as a "problem," and the success of the project is often measured by how well the team produced the original specified deliverables according to time and cost estimates generated.

In a perfect world where customers and project teams had psychic powers and 20-20 foresight, the waterfall approach might work. In the real world, customers often fail to communicate key requirements (or the project team fails to capture those requirements), priorities or technologies change, or competitive pressures necessitate reevaluation of requirements. In fact, sometimes producing the originally designated deliverables is entirely inappropriate by the time the project is over.

E-learning project management requires a more dynamically flexible approach, one that will serve you and your e-learning audience more efficiently and more effectively.

THE POWER OF AN EVOLUTIONARY PHILOSOPHY

If you use an evolutionary philosophy to manage your e-learning projects, you start out with a solid set of requirements, but you also recognize from the very beginning that changes are not only inevitable but desirable as well. You and your e-learning customer will discover both new requirements and requirements that were initially overlooked. What were previously high-priority items will no longer be the most important.

Your job as project manager is to work with your customer to deliver a final product that includes the most important deliverables. To do so requires an adaptive approach to allow you and the customer to negotiate changes in priorities. You will need to create a process that will have the maximum flexibility without deteriorating into chaos. You'll need to structure your project so that everyone involved receives ongoing feedback about your progress and knows at which key points in the project you are able to deal with changes in requirements. At each of these points, the final set of requirements becomes clearer and clearer. Your final product, therefore, evolves from its initial definition and becomes finally clear in the last of the points described.

E-Learning Project Development Cycle

The e-learning project development cycle lets you define your e-learning product initially, identify its key features, and break the project into a series of time-boxed delivery points for introducing those features. Each delivery point prior to final delivery reexamines the remaining features and allows for new priorities and substitution of new features. Here, in summary, is a seven-step approach for e-learning projects:

1. *Concept:* You'll work with your customer to identify the elements that your e-learning product should contain. This step is largely dedicated to researching available resources, the product desired, learning objectives to be met, technical considerations for e-learning delivery, and so forth. Determine the forms of documentation you propose to use in the project and have them ready to present at the product definition session.

2. *Product definition session:* This meeting is the first facilitated joint session you hold with your team and the customers for whom you're developing the e-learning course. You'll identify the key features for your e-learning product, giving you and your customer a preliminary vision of the e-learning product. At this session you also introduce documentation standards and forms to be used throughout the project. When you're done with this session, everyone involved will know the primary purpose of the e-learning product; the intended audience; the key features of the product and preliminary assessment of the relative priority of those features; specific innovative features to be introduced and key user interface requirements; and minimum hardware and software requirements for e-learners participating in the course.

3. *Initial cycle planning:* Immediately following the definition of your e-learning product, you develop a plan for delivering the features you've identified at the product definition session. Your plan breaks the project delivery timeframe into a small number of cycles of fixed duration (say, 3 to 6 weeks) and indicates which features are to be delivered at the end of each cycle. It also spells out how the project will deal with priority changes during each cycle and at the end of each cycle.

4. *Development cycles and interim delivery sessions:* You and your team create a working version of the e-learning product that will deliver the features earmarked for delivery in the first cycle. The cycle culminates in another joint session with your team and the customers to demonstrate the product's functionality and to identify any changes to those features. Each of these sessions is devoted to evaluating and prioritizing remaining features in the product and allows for negotiations to add new features—either at the expense of features that can be eliminated or at the cost of additional development costs and time. Then, at the penultimate session, all parties will reach agreement about which features are to be delivered at the end of the last cycle.

5. *Product acceptance:* The last cycle completes the delivery of the agreed-upon e-learning product. A final acceptance session verifies that the final list of features has been delivered and that the e-learning product is ready for rollout.

6. *Product rollout:* This phase integrates the e-learning product into your organization's existing e-learning curriculum.

7. *Project retrospective:* This phase evaluates the success of the project, identifies best practices and lessons learned for future e-learning projects, and points out risks that could threaten future projects.

The e-learning project development cycle becomes more complex as the size of the project increases. Generally speaking, the "product" metaphor is the recommended approach for delivering e-learning. You'll see how you can sell this approach to your organization in coming chapters.

Secrets of Keeping E-Learning Customers Involved

Keeping your e-learning customers and stakeholders involved throughout the project is possibly the biggest challenge you will face as project manager. However, the cycle approach just described has a number of elements designed to involve your customers and keep them providing meaningful input to your e-learning project.

One such opportunity is the formal product definition session. Everyone involved will have a true picture of the finished e-learning product by the end of this session. They will also have a clear understanding of roles and responsibilities for turning that picture into a reality. No project should be allowed to proceed without a commitment of one customer liaison who either will be on the product development team or will be readily available on a frequent (preferably daily) basis once the project moves forward.

In addition, customers can see the actual, working features at each interim delivery session. The two or three interim delivery sessions ensure that your customers have a clear picture of the evolving e-learning product. These sessions also help maintain momentum as you demonstrate key features. Between sessions, the customer liaison provides feedback to the customer sponsors and to the development team. Lines of communication will stay open because there is active involvement through a dedicated (or at least designated) customer representative.

You can keep your e-learning product in the limelight by marketing it just as though you were selling it outside the walls of your organization. This approach may sound as though it is outside the scope of a project manager's responsibility, but nothing is more effective in managing expectations than frequent, targeted reporting of your progress toward delivering your e-learning product to the customer. Obviously, your weekly reports are your first mode of communication, but do all you can to keep your project visible to all stakeholders.

E-Learning Project Launches

Your e-learning project starts out as a way to solve some specific problem for your organization. It moves from concept to vision at the product definition session. Having the right people attend this session is critical to the eventual success of your e-learning project. You might even want to think of planning and running the product definition session as the first subproject to be completed in the overall e-learning project.

The Ongoing Role of Review in E-Learning

Whatever your current e-learning project—be it a pilot project or a project to add another e-learning product to your e-learning environment—you must plan to use the review process to identify lessons learned, mistakes to avoid, and pitfalls to sidestep in future projects. If this e-learning project is the first one for your organization, then have your team members look back to other course development or technical projects they have tackled. If you've already started your e-learning initiative, then your team can learn from previous e-learning projects. Always look back before moving forward! Take a couple of hours to brainstorm with your team about past projects and what all of you can learn from your collective experiences. Ask the same questions you'll ask at the end of this new project. You will not only provide your team with a common ground of understanding, you'll also lay the foundation for a successful post-project review.

Continuous Improvement in E-Learning

To be successful as an e-learning project manager, you'll need to steer your project from inception to completion using a flexible adaptive process. Each cycle ends in an interim delivery session and reevaluation of the remaining features to be delivered. After each session, make sure you meet with your team to examine how you can improve your delivery of the next set of features. This doesn't have to be a formal session, but be prepared to modify your plan, add or delete tasks based on lessons learned, and make it a goal to improve your team's performance in each successive cycle.

TIME-BOXED E-LEARNING PROJECT MANAGEMENT

The cycle-based approach just described is dramatically different from traditional project management approaches you may have used in the past. We *don't* want to send you off into a new venture as e-learning project manager without reexamining traditional project management practices. We *do* want to help you apply those practices in effective new ways that we believe are conducive to greater success in delivering products such as e-learning courses. We started with an overview of a new approach. Now, let's get back to basics before we delve deeper into how to manage e-learning projects.

YOUR TURN

At the end of every chapter, you'll find a few simple exercises to help you to get started applying some of the e-learning project management principles you've read about here to your own organization's e-learning efforts. If you prefer not to write in this book, you can download copies of these exercises from the book's companion Website (www.projectmanagingelearning.com). Remember, there are no right or wrong answers; your situation is unique. Nevertheless, taking time to work through these activities should help you identify e-learning project management solutions that are appropriate to your situation.

Based on your current level of experience with e-learning and with project management, identify on worksheet 1-1 a few of the specific skills you'd like to acquire to help you with your e-learning projects.

Review the section in this chapter on why e-learning projects fail. Pick three or four of these pitfalls and see if you can think of some ways to help avoid them in your e-learning project (worksheet 1-2). Who can help you sidestep these pitfalls?

Worksheet 1-1. What do you need to learn about project management of e-learning?

New E-Learning Project Management Skill You Want to Attain	When You Want to Have This Skill	Done? (✔)

Worksheet 1-2. Avoiding e-learning project pitfalls.

Pitfall	How Can You Sidestep This Pitfall?	Who Can Help?	Discussed With Another Member of My Organization (✔)

If you agree that keeping your customer involved throughout your entire e-learning project is essential to producing a great e-learning product, brainstorm several additional ways of keeping their attention during your projects (worksheet 1-3). Select one or two of these and indicate when you have actually implemented them.

Worksheet 1-3. Additional ways of keeping the customer involved.

Idea for Keeping Customer Involved Throughout the Project	Date Implemented

2

Project Management 101 Applied to E-Learning

Even if you've never actually studied the discipline of project management, you may already have an intuitive grasp of many of the principles and practices used to see that assignments are completed on time and within budget. At the same time, you'll find that reviewing and adapting basic project management concepts to the world of e-learning course development can give you a better idea of which principles you can use "out of the box" and which ones need to be adapted for successful e-learning project management.

THE DISCIPLINE DEFINED

Project management is the discipline of applying information, talent, tools, and techniques to meet a specified set of goals while taking into account constraints of costs, schedule, scope, risks, and quality issues. Projects have an identifiable beginning and an end; therefore, they are different from ongoing processes. Projects usually use temporary resources, that is, human, material, and financial resources made available only for the duration of the project. Project team members often report to others inside or outside the organization and are in effect "on loan" to the project manager—usually on a part-time basis.

VIRTUAL COLLABORATION

Even in conventional projects, project team members often work in geographically separate locations. In e-learning projects, such separation is even more common. The "e-learning project office" is seldom a real, physical suite of rooms. More likely it is a virtual office with communication taking place via telephone, email, collaborative Internet tools, and videoconferencing. It's not unusual for the team to encounter some of the challenges facing e-learners in their own experiences in trying to keep a sense of team and community throughout their first e-learning project.

THE PROCESS, THE PRODUCT, AND THE PROJECT

It is important to know how the e-learning process, e-learning products, and e-learning projects can be distinguished from one another.

The *e-learning process* is an overall strategy for providing knowledge to the organization's audiences (internal and external) using technology and connectivity (usually the Internet). An *e-learning product* is a discrete package obtained at the end of one specific e-learning project. The product may be a new course, a new learning module, or a new e-learning curriculum. It may be a new learning management system or physical platform for delivering e-learning. Later, an e-learning product could be a revised package coming out of an e-learning maintenance or enhancement project. Finally, an *e-learning project* is an initiative to deliver or enhance a discrete package of e-learning content or to create, install, or maintain software or infrastructure to support the e-learning process.

Your organization may have launched an e-learning initiative that ultimately will support internal staff, business partners, and customers. We must assume that from its inception, your e-learning process will be ongoing and will require resources and staffing to support it on an ongoing basis. Never call this an e-learning project! Once launched, your e-learning initiative becomes just as much a part of your organization's fundamental business strategy as information technology, telecommunications, and e-commerce.

You may decide that the first package of e-learning content will be basic help-desk training. Obviously, that package could range in size from something quite simple to something incredibly complex. However you define it, it will become Version 1.0 of your organization's e-learning for help-desk services. Version 1.0 will be the e-learning product that is to be created from your first e-learning content project. Assuming that Version 1.0 is a success, there will probably be a new project in the future to create Version 2.0. (Or, if the first version needs some tweaking, a small project to create Version 1.1 may be launched.)

The minute you stop making the distinction between product (what your project delivers) and project (the e-learning deliverable), your organization's e-learning process is destined to become mired in perpetually unfinished projects and shoddy, poorly executed products. Remember that the e-learning process *never* ends; e-learning projects have a clearly defined beginning and end; and e-learning products evolve through a series of discrete construction and enhancement projects.

THE FOUR MAJOR STAGES OF A PROJECT

Lou Russell (2000) uses a four-stage approach to project management:

- *Define:* the stage in which the project charter is created, the specific objectives and deliverables for the project are spelled out, risks are identified, and change management procedures are agreed upon.
- *Plan:* the stage in which required tasks are identified, effort and cost estimates are made, and a project schedule and budget are approved and published.
- *Manage:* the stage in which tasks are executed, risks to the project are managed, and scope and change control procedures are administered.
- *Review:* the stage during which team and stakeholders formally evaluate the success of the project, publish their findings, and turn over project documentation to the quality assurance group.

The seven steps to an e-learning project were introduced in chapter 1. As shown in table 2-1, these steps can be nested into Russell's four stages.

WHAT'S DIFFERENT ABOUT E-LEARNING PROJECTS?

E-learning projects generally demand rapid deployment and high quality. These demands mean that you normally won't have the luxury of lengthy needs assessments and requirements definition. E-learning products also

Table 2-1. Nesting the seven steps for an e-learning project into Russell's (2000) four stages of project management.

Russell's Project Management Stages	Seven Steps for E-Learning Projects
Define	1. Concept: What problem does this project address? 2. Product definition session: How might it look? Who will build it?
Plan	3. Initial cycle planning: Schedule delivery cycles and interim delivery sessions
Manage	4. Development cycles and interim delivery sessions: Creation and time-boxed delivery of e-learning product features; revised cycle plans and reprioritization of features 5. Product acceptance: Final delivery session 6. Product rollout: Deployment of e-learning product in the working environment
Review	7. Project retrospective: Formal review of product success, project management lessons learned, overall review of state of e-learning process within the organization

require flexible content and a learner-friendly interface design. To keep pace with rapid deployment demands, your prototypes need to be *working* prototypes not just *models* to be discarded and replaced with "the real thing" later. This is where the cyclical approach comes in.

Each cycle gets you closer to a completed e-learning product and at the same time allows you to demonstrate real working "builds" of your product so that your e-learning customers experience using the product before it is completed. This way, they can periodically reevaluate and assign new priorities to product features along the way. This kind of project management requires a high degree of trust between e-learning customers and e-learning product developers, a firm grasp of risk management techniques and negotiating skills, as well as an ability to manage multiple activities within very tight timeframes.

YOUR TURN

Use the following activities to help apply some of the principles outlined in this chapter to your organization's e-learning initiative. Consider the current state of e-learning within your organization and where you think you are headed in the immediate future.

First, using worksheet 2-1, consider the overall environment for your organization's e-learning initiative.

Worksheet 2-1. Current state of e-learning management.	
Who is already involved or soon will be involved in delivering and managing e-learning within your organization?	
Where are they located?	
What challenges do you face in keeping the lines of communication open among all these people?	
Are your geographic locations such that you can all meet at least using telephone or videoconferencing for real-time interaction, or are you so widely separated by time zones that some individuals will have to get up in the middle of the night to participate?	
Will team members and stakeholders for a specific project also be widely distributed?	

Next, use worksheet 2-2 to examine the current overall e-learning delivery process.

Worksheet 2-2. Current state of the e-learning delivery process.

For the e-learning currently in place or under development, who is responsible for the e-learning process?	
Who maintains the Website? Who monitors Web traffic for e-learning courses?	
Who is responsible for backing up and archiving e-learning courses?	
Who carries out long-range planning for future e-learning expansion?	
Who monitors your e-learning program for learner satisfaction?	
Who evaluates new Web development and e-learning course development tools for purchase or upgrade?	

Now, take a look at the current e-learning products (courses and so forth) being produced within your organization (worksheet 2-3).

Worksheet 2-3. Current state of e-learning products.

What e-learning *products* are currently deployed within your organization?	
Is there a specific *curriculum* defined with at least one or more courses planned or implemented (for example, customer service, sales, and so forth)?	
Name a specific course that is already in place or that will be in place in the near future. (Call this Version 1.0 of the course.)	
Identify a couple of new features you might include in Version 2.0 of the course you named above.	

Finally, examine what might be on the horizon for e-learning initiatives within your organization (worksheet 2-4).

Worksheet 2-4. Potential future e-learning project initiatives.

What types of e-learning *projects* might be under consideration in the near future in your organization?	
Think of a project to create a new e-learning course offering.	
Think of an e-learning project to create a major new version of an existing course.	
Think of an e-learning project to install a major upgrade to the infrastructure supporting your organization's e-learning offerings.	
Think of an e-learning project to train your organization's e-learning course developers in the use of a new e-learning tool. (Note: This project is to deliver training to your course developers. The training that is the deliverable may or may not necessarily be Web-based! It may, in fact, be a hands-on workshop in a typical computer training room environment.)	

3

Stage 1: Defining the Project

Sometimes called the project charter, the e-learning project definition is your "license" to do business as a project team. When you define your e-learning project, you identify

- the problem to be solved (or the opportunity to be seized!)
- a vision of the finished e-learning product and its principal features
- the project objectives that translate this vision into a concrete set of deliverables to produce to complete the project and solve the problem
- the scope of the product itself
- the scope of the project itself, with definitions of roles and responsibilities of all parties involved
- the relative priorities of time, cost, and quality/scope
- the risks that might threaten the project
- the overall method you'll use for collaboration and how you'll manage change during the execution of the project
- how you plan to communicate progress to all of the stakeholders in the project.

STATING THE PROBLEM

The problem statement spells out the *why* behind your e-learning project. It points to the problem to be solved, the opportunity to be seized, or the need to be met as a result of completing of your e-learning project. Here are a couple of examples:

- *Example 1:* Currently, the call center receives more than 1,000 calls per day. Nearly 12 percent of these calls never actually reach a call center service representative because customers left on hold hang up before being routed to the representative. Studies show that calls involving defective products and product returns take almost twice as much customer representative time as other types of calls. Therefore, a training solution is needed for the call center that will concentrate on product returns and refund/replacement policies. This training must be individualized and should require no travel on the part of participants.

■ *Example 2:* The Jones County School System spends more than $75,000 each summer to offer remedial courses in English composition and math for students hoping to enter their senior year and receive their diplomas before the end of the coming school year. Many of these students need to work over the summer to help support their families at home and would benefit from course offerings available for study at any time of day or night. What is needed is a solution to meet this need and at the same time reduce the current delivery costs from $75,000 to $50,000 for the first summer. The ultimate goal is to bring these costs down to $25,000 or less in subsequent summers.

You probably can see that both of these problem statements seem to cry out for e-learning solutions. However, always remember that other solutions may work just as well. After all, to the handyman who only owns a hammer, everything looks like a nail! Make sure the project objectives you create truly address the problem as it appears in your problem statement.

Needs Analysis in the Age of E-Learning

In developing your e-learning problem statement, you have started to discover the potential solutions. This formal exploration, or needs analysis, eventually maps to a set of objectives that will attempt to fill the gaps identified in the problem statement. Whether you are thinking of creating an e-learning solution from scratch, outsourcing the course development process, or buying an e-learning course or module off-the-shelf, it's useful to have a strong mental picture—or vision—of your e-learning product.

Product Scope Versus Project Scope

The most powerful tool for delineating the boundaries of your e-learning solution is the product context diagram. This graphic shows at a glance what your finished product delivers, what it expects from outside its boundaries, who interacts with the product, and how it interacts with other systems. Figure 3-1 shows the components for creating a product context diagram.

There is a second, equally powerful tool that you, as an e-learning project manager, may wish to introduce: the project context diagram. Figure 3-2 shows the components for creating the project context diagram. The *project* context diagram depicts your project team's interactions with key individuals, organizations, and systems outside the project to meet your project objectives—in contrast to the *product* context diagram, which defines how your finished product should function. Figure 3-3 shows the product context diagram for an e-learning course to support sales staff in a chain of video stores. Figure 3-4 shows the project context diagram for a project team responsible for creating an orientation course on payroll procedures.

Figure 3-1. Components of a product context diagram.

My E-Learning Product	Your e-learning solution, usually drawn as a rounded-corner square, and always in the center of the graphic
Any Individuals or Organizations Interacting With My E-Learning Product	One rectangle for each class of individual (e.g., student) or organization (e.g., HR) that might interact with the e-learning product
Systems That Interact With My E-Learning Product	One rectangle (with an extra line inside the top) for each class of system (e.g., your learning management system) that may interact with your e-learning product
⟶	One arrow for each major class of information that flows to or from your e-learning product

Figure 3-2. Components of a project context diagram.

My E-Learning Project	The name of the e-learning project, usually appearing in the center of the graphic as a rounded-corner square
Any Individuals or Organizations Interacting With My E-Learning Project Team	One rectangle for each class of individual (e.g., project sponsor) or organization (e.g., "IT Department") that may interact with your e-learning project team in developing your product
Systems That Interact With My E-Learning Project Team	One rectangle (with an extra line inside the top) for each class of system (e.g., a course module library) that be used by your e-learning project team when developing the e-learning product
⟶	One arrow for each major class of information that flows to or from your e-learning project team

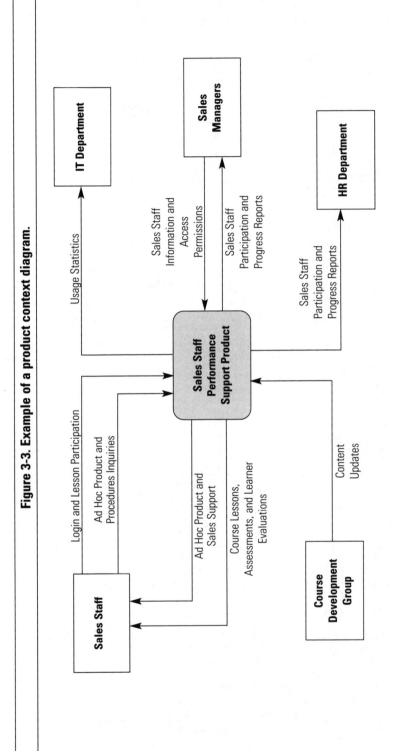

Figure 3-3. Example of a product context diagram.

Figure 3-4. Example of a project context diagram.

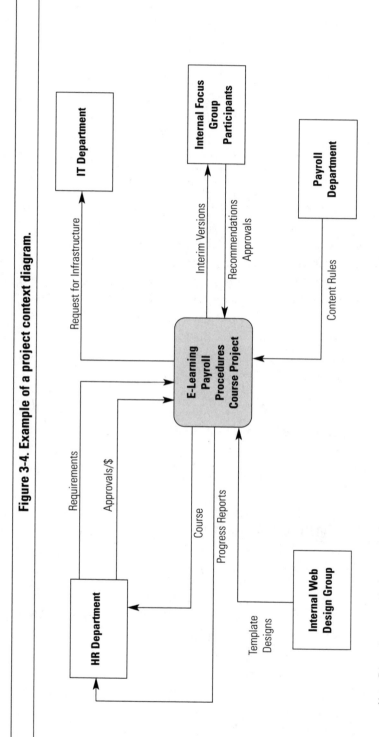

Note: E-Learning course designers are part of project team.

DEFINING PRIORITIES AND CONSTRAINTS

In an ideal world, every e-learning project would finish in the shortest possible time, would stay well under budget, and would have every conceivable feature included—all of the highest possible quality. In the real world of finite resources, you'll need to set priorities and manage time and resources to deliver the best product possible while honoring constraints of time, cost, and quality/scope. These three aspects can be represented by a triangle (figure 3-5).

If any of the three sides changes in size, the other sides must adjust to accommodate. For instance, adding new features will add more time or greater costs—or both. At the beginning of your e-learning project, you and your customer need to reach agreement about targets for time, cost, and scope/quality. Always use a tool like the priority matrix (figure 3-6) to establish which target is most important, which one is second in importance, and which target has the lowest priority. If the first two targets *must be met at all costs,* then the third target may or may not be attainable. As project manager, your planning and day-to-day management of the e-learning project depends on these priorities to make decisions as the project progresses. Your reporting on progress should always address these targets, and your customers need to constantly reassess the original priorities to see whether they still reflect their needs.

Figure 3-7 shows an example of a priority matrix for a specific e-learning project. This project must deliver an e-learning course by March 1. Second, there is already an established standard for the learning objectives for this course. With both of these constraints in place, it may not be possible to deliver the course within the $50,000 budget target. Your initial planning for the project will determine how close to the third target you may realistically come.

Figure 3-5. The triangle of project management.

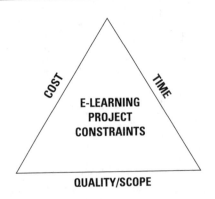

Figure 3-6. Priority matrix.

Target	1	2	3	Measurement
Time				
Cost				
Quality/Scope				

Figure 3-7. An example of a priority matrix for XYZ's online course.

Target	1	2	3	Measurement
Time	✔			Course must be available for new hires brought in for orientation on March 1.
Cost			✔	Total development costs should not exceed $50,000.
Quality/Scope		✔		Course must cover all skill sets required for Level 1 Certification as established by HR Document #CC1352.

THE ROLE OF RISK MANAGEMENT

Mastering the mechanics of project management is relatively straightforward. Too often, however, project managers ignore the "gotcha's" that plague virtually every project, those things that shouldn't go wrong but sometimes do in real-world projects. Risk management and change management are the two primary tools for anticipating and responding to threats to your e-learning project. There are five steps for building a solid risk management strategy into your e-learning project plan. These are described in the sections that follow.

1. Anticipate Hazards

Work with your project team and subject matter experts (SMEs) to identify what might possibly go wrong during the execution of your project. If you have completed other e-learning projects, you can reexamine the project review documents of previous projects to see if anything went wrong. Chances are, similar risks may exist for the current e-learning project as well.

Next, brainstorm as many likely (and unlikely) risks to your e-learning project with your team and SMEs. Encourage wild speculation and try to identify relatively harmless-sounding risks in these short sessions. You'll be surprised how many so-called unlikely events turn out to be genuine project risks and how many "minor irritation" risks turn out to be major roadblocks later on. Better to identify too many risks than leave some out at this point.

2. Assess the Risks to Your Project

Take your list of risks and score each one on a scale of 1 to 3, with 3 being the highest. For each risk, assess

- the likelihood of occurrence (How likely is this risk to occur during the execution of your e-learning project?)
- overall impact (How serious are the consequences of this risk if it occurs?)
- degree of control (How much direct influence do you have to keep this risk from occurring?).

Then, create a risk index using this formula:

$$\text{Risk Index} = \frac{(\text{Likelihood of Occurrence}) \times (\text{Overall Impact})}{(\text{Degree of Control})}$$

The formula takes into account that risks with the least likelihood of occurring (score = 1), with low impact (score = 1), and over which you have a high degree of control (score = 3) are the ones that pose the least threat to the project. In contrast, risks that have a high likelihood (score = 3), that will have a high impact if they occur (score = 3), and over which you have very little control (score = 1) are the most threatening to your e-learning project.

For most projects, scope creep is a common risk, with high scores for likelihood of occurrence (score = 3), and overall impact (score = 3), but with a high degree of control as well (score = 3). Therefore, the index would be:

$$\frac{3 \times 3}{3} = 3$$

On the other hand, in troubled times, a nationwide disruption of Internet services might be a likely event (score = 3), with high impact (score = 3), and something over which you have little control (score = 1) would receive the highest possible index:

$$\frac{3 \times 3}{1} = 9$$

Your brainstorming sessions will also yield a few items such as "project manager forgets to bring donuts," which is highly unlikely (score = 1), will have minimal impact (score = 1), and you have available many ways to remind the project manager to perform this task (score = 1). Therefore, its index is

$$\frac{1 \times 1}{1} = 1$$

3. Assign Priorities to the Risks

After you have identified potential risks and calculated risk indexes for each, list the risks in descending order of risk. Those appearing at the top of the list are the ones that require your greatest attention. Table 3-1 is an example of a ranked list.

4. Managing Risks

For the highest-scoring risks, determine what actions might be taken to prevent them from occurring and what contingencies might be put into place for dealing with them if they actually do occur. Everyone talks about managing risks as part of project management. The bad news is that actually taking the necessary steps to prevent adverse occurrences and to put together contingency plans costs time and money. Recognizing risks is only half the battle; dealing with them as a project manager is the more difficult half.

5. What Will It Cost?

Estimate the time and costs required for implementing preventive measures and contingency plans, decide which ones you will implement, and build them into your final project plan. Managing risks is like buying insurance and

Table 3-1. Sample list of risks and associated risk indexes.

Risk	Likelihood (1–3)	Impact (1–3)	Control (1–3)	Risk Index (1–9)
Disruption of Internet services prevents learners from participating.	3	3	1	9
Course development software is buggy.	2	3	1	6
Project costs exceed estimate.	2	3	1	6
Scope creep occurs.	3	3	3	3
Subject matter experts (SMEs) are not available when needed.	1	3	1	3
Competitors provide similar course offerings free or at lower cost.	1	3	1	3
Learner workstations are slow.	2	2	2	2
Project manager forgets to bring donuts to meeting.	1	1	1	1

includes paying premiums out of your e-learning project resources. Can you choose not to pay the premiums? Of course, but the consequences for not having insurance are grave. You and your project sponsors must balance the need for adequate coverage with the need to control project costs. Managing every risk can drain valuable resources better spent on delivering your e-learning product; not investing in preventive measures for those risks that threaten your project the most can lead to disaster for your e-learning project.

THE ROLE OF CHANGE MANAGEMENT

Every e-learning project involves some sort of change. Change management is the process of

- facilitating acceptance and implementation of intended changes (what should be different when your e-learning product is in place)
- responding to unexpected changes in project requirements (what is truly necessary and what is the cost to provide)
- averting undesirable changes (unnecessary changes to scope of your e-learning product or delivery method).

The cornerstone of good change management skills is the ability to manage expectations among your project's stakeholders. This process starts at the project definition stage, where you define scope and objectives and spell out how you will deal with risks. You can facilitate acceptance and implementation of intended changes by keeping all involved informed about the product your e-learning project will deliver, how you're delivering it, and the expected benefits for the learners and those who hold a stake in the success of the learners. You can set the stage for handling necessary changes in requirements by spelling out the process whereby additional features can be made available in exchange for additional expenditures of time and cost or giving up other less urgently needed features. You can help avoid many undesirable changes through a risk management process like the one spelled out in the above section. A risk management strategy designed to preempt setbacks to your e-learning project (or at least respond decisively to them when they occur) is your best possible approach to averting undesirable changes.

DEFINING THE COLLABORATIVE ENVIRONMENT

A successful e-learning project requires an environment designed to enable and encourage collaboration among all parties involved in the creation of an e-learning product. Just as effective e-learning is always *learner focused,* effective e-learning projects are *product focused;* that is, you and the project team should avoid tightly defined role definitions in favor of a shared commitment to delivering an e-learning product of the highest possible quality on time and within budget. Members of collaborative teams share a vision of the final product, and they share credit and responsibility both for creating an e-learning product and for constantly improving the way they go about completing e-learning projects—and projects in general. For total success in e-learning projects, this kind of commitment is required not just of the official project team but of all stakeholders connected with your organization's e-learning effort.

DEFINING THE PROGRESS COMMUNICATION PLAN

Every e-learning project definition must include a table listing all levels of stakeholders for the project and the specific progress reports they each will receive. The frequency of each progress report and the depth of detail included in it should be appropriate to each level of stakeholder. Executive sponsors will not want to see progress reported in minute detail and will often only need

> ## Seven Characteristics of True Collaborative Environments
>
> 1. project kick-offs that stress the importance of collaboration and highlight successes and challenges from previous efforts
> 2. orientation into the concept that all involved in the e-learning project share a vision of the final product
> 3. customers' understanding of the time/cost/quality triangle and the necessity of reestimating projects when requirements change
> 4. participation of the customer, team, and stakeholders in interim review sessions where they evaluate interim versions of the final e-learning product
> 5. interim evaluations of the product including an evaluation of the collaboration process and an examination of how to improve the process for the next phase of the project
> 6. agreement between the e-learning course developers and the customer to give up the "us versus them" mentality. The customer is an ex officio team member, participating in the development, testing, implementation, and evaluation of the e-learning product under construction.
> 7. a formal evaluation of the e-learning product, its delivery, and the collaborative process, including recommendations to inform future projects.

to look at reports once or twice a month; your team members need to see both the big picture and the microview, requiring weekly—even daily—updates.

Try to define the reports and frequency of delivery as early as possible in your e-learning project and avoid deviating from the schedule. (Progress report delivery slippages are almost always a sign that the project is in some kind of trouble.) Consider an internal e-learning newsletter or your intranet as forums for delivering progress reports that are not of a sensitive nature.

YOUR TURN

Consider the last project you were involved in. (If you have not yet been involved in an e-learning project, then use another course development project or a software development project, depending upon your experience.) Based on your understanding of the priorities of the project, complete a priority matrix for the project (worksheet 3-1).

Worksheet 3-1. Priority matrix.

Target	1	2	3	Measurement
Time				
Cost				
Quality/Scope				

Explain why you think these were the priorities:

Consider this suggestion: If you know others who were involved in the same project, ask them to complete the worksheet independently and compare your results with theirs. (You may be in for a surprise!)

Next, take 2 minutes to brainstorm 15 risks you may encounter on your next e-learning project. Don't be afraid to come up with some improbable or even silly ones in this exercise. The main point is to generate ideas and list them on worksheet 3-2.

Worksheet 3-2. Risk identification.

	Risk
1	
2	
3	
4	
5	
6	
7	
8	
9	
10	
11	
12	
13	
14	
15	

Now for each of the 15 e-learning project risks you identified, calculate on worksheet 3-3 the risk indexes using the formula introduced in this chapter.

Worksheet 3-3. Risk scoring and prioritization.				
Risk	**Likelihood 1–3**	**Impact 1–3**	**Control 1–3**	**Risk Index 1–9**
1				
2				
3				
4				
5				
6				
7				
8				
9				
10				
11				
12				
13				
14				
15				

As you look back over the risks on worksheet 3-3, circle the four top-scoring items in the list. For each of the four top risks, indicate on worksheet 3-4 some actions you and your organization can take to avoid the risk. Indicate at least one action that can be taken if the risk actually occurred.

Worksheet 3-4. Risk management activities.

Risk # _____

Three activities to help avoid this risk:

1.

2.

3.

Action(s) to take if the risk occurs:

Risk # _____

Three activities to help avoid this risk:

1.

2.

3.

Action(s) to take if the risk occurs:

Risk # _____

Three activities to help avoid this risk:

1.

2.

3.

Action(s) to take if the risk occurs:

Risk # _____

Three activities to help avoid this risk:

1.

2.

3.

Action(s) to take if the risk occurs:

4

Stage 2: Planning the E-Learning Project

Once you've defined your e-learning project and the e-learning product your project will generate, build your project plan to determine the activities necessary to create the product, the human and material resources required to complete those activities, and the associated schedule and budget for completing the project. This chapter describes how to develop a project plan and its components.

If you've done a good job of defining your e-learning project, then you have a solid basis for creating a realistic project plan. Your e-learning project definition provides a set of objectives that you now can translate into project deliverables—each one of which will require time and resources to produce. The clearer your project objectives, the more concrete each deliverable becomes and the easier it is to break it into components and define activities to produce those components.

E-LEARNING PROJECT MILESTONES

Milestones are like points in geometry. Milestones are activities that have no length in terms of duration, yet they mark important boundaries that define your e-learning project. Activities that complete the creation of a course, a lesson, or a topic should all culminate in a final milestone, sometimes simply given a designation "Course Created" or "Lesson Created" or "Topic Created." Other important milestones would include key changes of status of the product, such as "Lesson Ready for Final Team Testing." A subsequent milestone would be "Lesson Tested and Ready for Final Cycle Review Approval."

You determine these milestones by

■ enumerating the components of each deliverable and identifying activities (including auxiliary activities) required to produce each component

- sequencing activities logically, taking into account activity dependencies
- estimating the duration required to complete each activity based on use of a single resource and adjusting each activity's duration, taking into account the number of resources available
- setting time-boxed delivery cycles to determine when all components will be completed for each deliverable based on the working schedule of the project team.

Enumerating Deliverable Components and Identifying Activities

Your first task, when developing a project plan for your e-learning project, is to determine the deliverables and break each of the deliverables into sets of components to be produced. In the example shown in figure 4-1, the hierarchical breakdown gives a picture of the components for each type of deliverable in a customer service curriculum. Start with the double-bordered item, and trace its components to the lowest level of the diagram.

Every project consists of not only activities to produce deliverables but also auxiliary activities to help keep the project on track. These include

- reporting activities
- change management activities
- risk management activities
- delivery cycle review activities
- other administrative activities such as publication of lessons learned, updating of schedules, and so forth.

Sequencing Activities

Once you've identified all the activities to be performed in your project, determine which activities depend on others to complete and see which ones can be performed at the same time. There are several kinds of activity dependencies:

- *Mandatory dependencies:* Some activities can only be performed after another activity is completed. For instance, in an office move, you can't move in the furniture until the carpet is installed.
- *Discretionary dependencies:* You can decide the order of activities that fall into this category. For example, you have the option of creating the documentation for an e-learning course before producing the course lessons so that the documentation drives course development rather than the other way around.
- *External dependencies:* These dependencies may be mandated because certain resources will only be available later. For instance, testing may be delayed until the quality assurance team becomes available. Similarly,

Figure 4-1. An example of how to break down e-learning components.

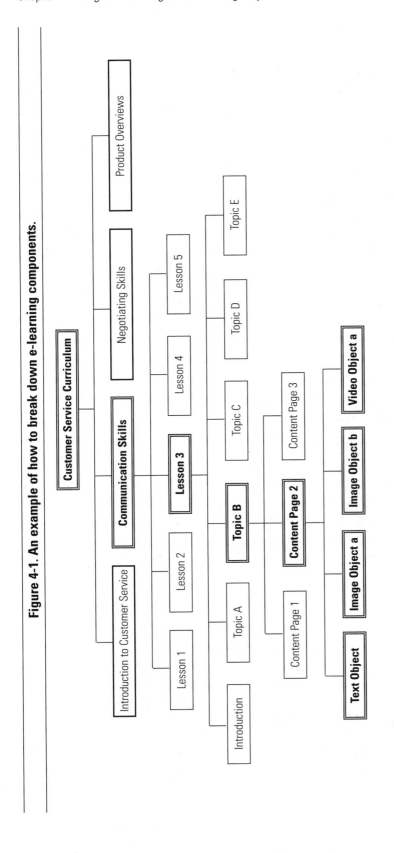

government agencies or accreditation agency requirements may necessitate producing certain deliverables before others.

■ *Cycle review dependencies:* These dependencies are a special kind of discretionary dependency. They stem from the need to deliver meaningful chunks of e-learning product at each cycle review session. Therefore, you may decide to accelerate completion of components of a deliverable to have sufficient functionality to demonstrate a portion of it at a review session.

Estimating Activity Durations

Estimate the number of hours it will take to complete each activity identified. Chapter 10 will show you how to create realistic estimates for your project activities and sequence them for your project. Keep your preliminary estimate figures and compare them with the actual effort required to complete each item. Don't be surprised if your first project shows a wide variance between estimated and actual. However, the duration data from your first project should help you do a much better job of estimating on your next e-learning project. Continue to compare estimated and actual figures over several projects, and make it a goal to narrow the gap between the two sets of figures.

Setting Time-Boxed Delivery Cycles

Because most e-learning projects are likely to have fixed delivery deadlines, use time-boxed delivery cycles to ensure on-time delivery and interim review of your e-learning product as it evolves. For example, if you need to have an e-learning course available in 90 days, you would divide the project into three 4-week delivery cycles, each culminating in a delivery cycle review. A 6-month e-learning project may be divided into four cycles of 6 weeks' duration. Each cycle would deliver working components of the final product and a means of demonstrating how that final product will work. This process is similar to prototyping but should, to the extent possible, contain working components that will be part of the final product.

CYCLE REVIEW SESSIONS

The major milestones for your e-learning project are marked by the delivery review sessions, which are fixed at the beginning of the project. Each delivery cycle review session demonstrates to the project customers and stakeholders the functionality of the e-learning product as it evolves. At the end of each cycle, the customers and stakeholders have an opportunity to evaluate the product components delivered thus far, reaffirm the appropriateness of the remaining components, and, possibly, request new features to be introduced in lieu of features currently scheduled for delivery in future cycles. Features requested in addition to currently scheduled features may require reestimation of the project and the appropriation of additional resources to deliver those features.

The cycle review sessions themselves entail a variety of project activities:

- scheduling the sessions
- setting up the room
- loading the demonstration courseware
- compiling the lessons learned, change request summaries, and other documentation resulting from the cycle review session.

To have meaningful cycle review sessions, you need to coordinate completion milestones with these sessions. In other words, whenever you have discretionary sequencing of activities, sequence the activities in such a way that course content and activities are available for demonstration and approval at each cycle review session. This may necessitate the introduction of additional milestones such as "Lesson Ready for Preliminary Demonstration" and "Lesson Ready for Preliminary Team Testing" prior to total completion of the module. In the cycle review session, only part of the lesson functionality would be available for demonstration—but enough to give a clear picture of what the final lesson would accomplish. Obviously, the next cycle review session would include a demonstration of the complete lesson.

IS PROJECT MANAGEMENT SOFTWARE FOR YOU?

If you are already adept at using project management software, such as Microsoft Project, then you will probably want to use it to enter your project activities and create sequencing networks. Increasingly, teams creating Web-based applications like e-learning products are using such software for creating the initial plans and for storing actual results for later reference, but they tend to rely more heavily on simpler methods of tracking progress. Figure 4-2 offers an example of an activity sequencing network for an e-learning project created using Microsoft Project's custom formatting features.

The time-boxed approach described here creates a framework for monitoring progress in a very real, very direct way. Each cycle review session is a highly visible indicator of project progress. Keeping the team focused on the delivery of a real, functional e-learning product rather than the completion of isolated tasks fosters a collaborative environment to deliver quality e-learning courses for your organization.

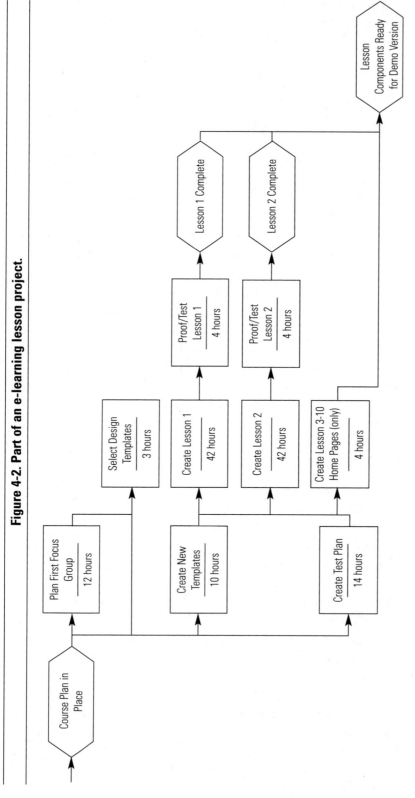

Figure 4-2. Part of an e-learning lesson project.

Your Turn

Your assignment is to create an online orientation minicourse for your department. It must be complete in one month! You will hold a 1-hour review session at the end of each of the next 3 weeks before making this orientation available to new employees. Use worksheet 4-1 to guide you through the steps to create this minicourse.

Worksheet 4-1. Mapping objectives to content and activities.

List three or four learning objectives for the orientation:

Objective 1:

Objective 2:

Objective 3:

Objective 4:

Identify content elements to cover these objectives. What activities might you use to help learners master this content?

Content for Objective 1

Activities:

Content for Objective 2

Activities:

Content for Objective 3

Activities:

Content for Objective 4

Activities:

Next, estimate the time it would take to create each content element and each activity. Make sure you add activities of 1 to 2 hours' duration for each week for team meetings, report preparation, and review session results.

Activity No.	Activity Description	Estimated Duration
Worksheet 4-2. Minicourse project estimates for content and activities.		
1		
2		
3		
4		
5		
6		
7		
8		
9		
10		
11		
12		
13		
14		
15		
16		

Copy each activity and its duration onto a sticky note. Taking into account any dependencies, sequence the activities and identify appropriate milestones so that you have something meaningful to demonstrate at each of the three minireview sessions prior to delivering the course at the end of the one-month period.

Use a large poster board, whiteboard, or flipchart page and sticky notes for this exercise.

5

Stage 3:
Managing the Project

In stage 1, you defined your e-learning project by identifying its objectives and translating them into a vision of an e-learning product and then described the collaborative environment in which your project team would be producing that product. In addition, you identified specific risks to the project and some potential means of avoiding or dealing with those risks. In stage 2, you turned this definition of product and process into a concrete plan—a sequence of specific activities required to produce the deliverables, to deal with some of the risks identified in stage 1, and to keep the stakeholders of the project informed of progress and involved in the evolution of the final product.

In stage 3, the actual project work begins. You, as e-learning project manager, have the responsibility of keeping the project on track, dealing with changes occurring along the way, and handling both anticipated and unanticipated threats that arise as your team develops, tests, and delivers the e-learning product.

COLLABORATION VERSUS COMMAND AND CONTROL

In the old days of project management, your job might have been simpler: You simply completed your project definition, obtained sign-offs, set up a plan to deliver what was defined, and delivered exactly what was described in the plan. Any changes along the way were deemed deviations from the plan—things to be avoided as much as possible. If you met the original objectives of the plan, your project was a "success," even if your customers hated the final product and refused to use it! This scenario, unfortunately, is hardly an exaggeration. The recent history of product development and IT application development is rife with such examples.

The tight delivery schedules for products such as Web-based applications and, now, e-learning require a different approach, one that demands not only traditional project management skills but also skills in collaboration and adaptation. In chapter 3, you read about the characteristics of collaborative environments. As the project manager in an e-learning project, you'll avoid the old "command and control" mentality and lead your team and your stakeholders in ways that

- emphasize ongoing self-evaluation of the team, its successes, and challenges to seek ways of doing things better
- make sure that everyone on the team stays constantly aware of the "metaphor" of the final product, its purpose, and how everyone is equally vested in its creation and success
- help customers understand that time/cost/quality triangles mean that changes are possible—even desirable—but that changes always come at a cost and require reevaluation of schedule, budget, and number of features delivered
- emphasize the importance of each interim review session and insist that customers, team, and stakeholders understand why their attendance and participation are critical to the success of the final product
- formalize the collaborative process by including an evaluation component in each interim review session
- watch for early warning signs of "us versus them" relationships between course developers and the customer
- try to involve the customer in all aspects of development of the e-learning product
- include sections on collaboration in the final project review evaluation document.

The time and effort required to maintain a collaborative environment is considerable, but you'll find that the benefits more than justify the costs.

EVOLUTIONARY PROCESSES

The American Heritage Dictionary of the English Language (2000) defines evolution as "a gradual process in which something changes into a different and usually more complex or better form." Perhaps an even better term would be *adaptation,* defined in the same dictionary as "something. . .that is changed or changes so as to become suitable to a new or special application or situation." Both views, however, embrace change as a positive force in the development of an entity.

Your e-learning product will undoubtedly go through a number of changes from the time you define it initially to the time it becomes part of your active e-learning environment. That's why it is so important to specify procedures for handling change during stage 1. Not only have you described the process in the project definition, you also have created a preliminary snapshot of the project and its priorities with the following five project management tools:

- *Product context diagram:* This graphic provided a functional overview of the final e-learning product and the information it would be providing and receiving from e-learning participants, those responsible for administering e-learning, and the stakeholders who would be receiving reports and statistics about its use.
- *Project context diagram:* This graphic showed who would be interacting with the project team and what information they would be providing and receiving.
- *Priority matrix:* This tool provided the initial view of the relative priorities of time, cost, and quality/scope and would be used to help make decisions as changes arose.
- *Risk management assessment:* This assessment identified current and potential threats to the project, along with steps to take to avert or respond to these threats.
- *Change management procedures:* These documents not only described how you would manage expectations throughout your organization but also established the protocols to be used to expedite decisions about changes to project deliverables.
- *Progress communication plan:* This plan specified project reporting cycles and defined specific kinds of reports and the audience for each.

By starting off your e-learning project with these tools in place, you have a basis for managing the project in a way that takes optimal advantage of adaptive changes as you and your team move closer and closer to the delivery of the final e-learning product.

Managing Changes to Objectives

Changes to project objectives are possibly the most difficult of all changes to manage. Changes to objectives often redefine both the *what* and the *why* of a project and, therefore, have even greater effects than mere changes in scope. Changes in objectives often lead to a complete rethinking of the e-learning project. For instance, an e-learning project that starts out as a simple employee orientation course and ends up as an important part of the organization's ongoing knowledge management initiative raises the ante considerably. It usually means having to bring in a different cast of characters as stakeholders and may require revisiting the entire project definition phase. If the changes in objectives turn out to be nothing more than changes in the *what,* then you really may be dealing with scope changes.

It's easy to determine the magnitude of changes in objectives by applying this simple rule: If the change in objectives necessitates revising the project context diagram (that is, if the cast of characters or responsibilities change), then the change in objectives may dictate a rethinking of the project. If the change in objectives necessitates only a revision of the product context diagram, you probably can consider it as a change in product scope.

Managing Changes to Product Scope

Changes in product scope mean that the product is going to do more things, provide more information, or handle more kinds of information. Changes in product scope change the list of features of the product. They also require a revision of the product context diagram.

More important, changes in scope require reexamination of the priority matrix and some decisions about cost, schedule, and the number of features to be delivered. Adding features costs time and resources, or, at the least, necessitates a trade-off for another feature originally included as part of the plan. It is, therefore, crucial to do everything possible to deliver "keepers" in each delivery cycle so that changes in subsequent cycles do not involve rework of previous portions of your e-learning product.

Managing Technological Changes

The same rapid explosion of technology that makes e-learning possible also adds to the complexity of your e-learning project. Adding a new e-learning product to your e-learning curriculum is sometimes like trying to change jet engines during a flight! The Web itself, course development tools, learning management systems, and the capabilities of learner workstations are all growing more sophisticated daily. You may find it necessary to reevaluate platforms, tools, and techniques in the middle of a project. You may be tempted to introduce a new productivity tool to save time only to find that its steep learning curve actually impedes your team's progress. Decisions about your organization's overall e-learning strategy may affect your project in midstream as well. Stay aware of these risks when tempted to introduce new technology in the middle of the project. If using new tools or techniques was part of your original plan, make sure you included learning-curve time for your team as you estimate the project's activity durations.

MONITORING AND REEVALUATING RISKS

As your project gets under way, you will find that your original list of risks can help you watch out for threats to the project. You will also find that some risks that originally seemed either unlikely (or likely but not threatening) now have become serious threats to your project. Your ongoing progress reports should always include an update on project risks and any new steps needed to be taken to deal with them. Your ability to anticipate these threats at the time you defined the project will help prepare your stakeholders for the unexpected, but don't be surprised when new risks pop up along the way. Your ability to communicate these threats and explain how you will tackle them can build trust and create an atmosphere of shared responsibility for delivering your e-learning product.

YOUR TURN

Divide and conquer. One of the most daunting tasks in establishing an e-learning project management initiative is putting some of the tools described here in place. Remember, you're not in this alone. Identify other individuals within your organization—perhaps in the IT department or within your organization's project management office, or elsewhere in the training department—who can assist you in developing and implementing some of these tools and techniques.

Worksheet 5-1. Internal resources for developing and implementing e-learning project management tools and techniques.

Tool or Technique	Who Can Help?	Date to Contact	Contacted (✓)
Context Diagramming			
Priority Matrix			
Risk Management			
Change Management			
Estimating			
Project Management Software			
Course Authoring Software			
Learning Management Systems			
Content Management Systems			
E-Learning Professional Organizations			
Joint Application Development (JAD) and Interim Review Session			

6

Stage 4:
Reviewing the Project

After defining your project in stage 1 and laying out the specific tasks, time estimates, and delivery schedule in stage 2, you and your team had the challenge of completing your e-learning project, dealing with changes and handling threats to your success as they came up in stage 3. Finally, the project reaches completion; you and your team turn over the deliverables and are ready to turn to other activities inside your organization. But, before you do, a final—and very important—stage remains: the project review.

Throughout the project you should have conducted minievaluations of your progress, lessons learned, ways of making the collaborative process work better in the future, and so forth. Now it's time for a more comprehensive last review to wrap up the current project and to continue to improve performance in future e-learning projects.

PROJECT REVIEWS AND ORGANIZATIONAL LEARNING

The purpose of a project review is twofold. First, it provides closure and important documentation related directly to the e-learning product delivered in the project. The project review session memorializes the particulars about the project, addresses deliverables, and identifies the individuals and business units directly involved in the project. Furthermore, the project review session identifies specific roadblocks encountered and ways you and your team were able to overcome them. It names any open issues that may need resolution or necessitate future maintenance projects.

Second, the project review session advances your organization's knowledge base about how best to manage e-learning projects. The most far-reaching benefit of a project review is its application to future e-learning project management. When you identify what worked well on your project, you are very likely also spelling out best practices for future projects. When you note some action taken during your project that didn't work well, you help subsequent project teams avoid that action. The unexpected challenges that arose in your project can be identified as potential risks in future projects. The technical advances and discoveries your team made can become part of the standard project toolkit. This way, project reviews take a pivotal role in your organization's strategy for continuous improvement in delivering e-learning.

PROJECT REVIEWS AND PROJECT TEAM BUILDING

Depending on the size of your e-learning project, the project review session should be a facilitated session running anywhere from 45 minutes to a few hours and should involve the same group of team members and project stakeholders who attended the interim cycle reviews.

Before the review session, distribute a questionnaire to all attendees, including your e-learning project team, who will receive a more detailed version of this questionnaire (see chapter 12). Then, meet with your team members to share their responses and come up with a composite document from the team's perspective. Many organizations use this same technique as a team-building activity at the beginning of a project. In this case, each team member could use the questionnaire to evaluate the last project they tackled.

In addition, have your team review the questionnaires received from stakeholders and create a similar composite document based on stakeholder responses. These two composite documents will be preliminary discussion documents for the formal review session.

REEVALUATION OF DELIVERABLES

Given the high volatility of e-learning content, your review session should try to revisit such issues as the projected shelf life for the current e-learning product, any "wish list" items identified, and any needed improvements to the product as delivered.

Most e-learning content is likely to require updating after a certain amount of time. Traditional academic subjects, such as history or writing techniques, usually do not require frequent updates, but such topics as customer service, organizational policies and procedures, and most technical subjects certainly do. Every product should have a date by which the content will be reviewed to ensure that it is still useful. As the number of e-learning products increases, so will the amount of time required to "restock" existing e-learning content.

Don't expect to be able to meet every need the first time around. Every successful product has a whole list of potential enhancements and new features pending for the next version. You, your stakeholders, and your project team will almost certainly identify some of these potential enhancements as you develop the e-learning product in your project. The review session allows you to catalog these enhancements for future projects involving the product.

The term *needed improvements* is used euphemistically to describe the things that are less than perfect in your e-learning product. Yes, glitches will occur despite your best efforts to deliver a bug-free e-learning product with smooth, elegant learner interfaces for presenting the most engaging, highly relevant content. Short of flaws that render the product unusable—which should have been addressed immediately before implementing the e-learning product—such imperfections need to be documented so that your maintenance project schedule can address them in the future.

BEST PRACTICES

Each time you undertake an e-learning project, you will attempt to use the best practices available. Some of these you learn from e-learning experts outside your organization. The body of knowledge about e-learning grows daily; by participating in professional organizations like ASTD, reading the literature of e-learning such as the books in this series, and becoming involved with local user groups, you can collect valuable suggestions about how best to manage your e-learning projects. You will begin to see that the e-learning project management experiences within your organization are among the most relevant sources for e-learning best practices. Your project review session, therefore, provides value that extends beyond the current project: It adds to a bank of knowledge that is unique to your organization, knowledge that will help speed up e-learning product delivery, improve e-learning product quality, and generally simplify the management of future e-learning projects.

CREATING AND MAINTAINING A RISK DATABASE

You've already seen how risk management can help keep your e-learning project on course. You started the project with a number of specific threats in mind and planned some activities to avoid those threats or to reduce the threat to your e-learning project. At the end of each phase, you reexamined the list of threats and updated your strategy for proceeding with the project, taking into account your actual experience to that point in the project and using a rating system like the one described in chapter 2.

More likely than not, you encountered other hurdles that you had not anticipated in your risk assessments along the way. These "gotcha's" were the risks you didn't take into account for your current project. The project review, however, allows you to record them as potential risks for future projects so that they can be managed more effectively in the future.

Over time you will identify dozens—if not hundreds—of risks. You and other e-learning project managers gain experience as you avoid or mitigate these risks and develop contingency plans for responding more effectively to them. Your organization should consider storing this information in a simple database so that e-learning project managers can have ready access to this information. Significant events that should trigger updating this database occur

■ when you finalize your initial e-learning project plan
■ when you update your risk assessment at the end of each cycle review session
■ as part of your final project review phase.

Your Turn

Identify specific sources in worksheet 6-1 to obtain historical and predictive indicators of risks you may want to include if you need to start building a risk database for e-learning projects. Over the next few weeks, check out these sources and obtain a list of at least three potential risks identified through each source.

Worksheet 6-1. Risk database scavenger hunt.

Source 1: Previous e-learning projects within your organization (If not applicable, go to source 2.)
Potential risks based on past experiences:
1.
2.
3.
4.
Source 2: Previous learning projects (not e-learning) within your organization
Potential risks based on past experiences:
1.
2.
3.
4.

Worksheet 6-1. Risk database scavenger hunt (continued).

Source 3: IT projects within your organization

Potential risks based on past experiences:

1.

2.

3.

4.

Source 4: Books and periodicals on e-learning

Potential risks (indicate source):

1.

2.

3.

4.

Source 5: Websites devoted to e-learning

Potential risks (indicate source):

1.

2.

3.

4.

Source 6: Professional meetings devoted to e-learning

Potential risks (indicate speaker or source):

1.

2.

3.

4.

Source 7: Informal discussions with colleagues in other organizations

Potential risks (indicate source, unless they need to remain anonymous):

1.

2.

3.

4.

Part 2
Setting the Stage for Your E-Learning Project

The two chapters in this section will be of special interest to those of you who are launching your first e-learning projects and as yet have not gone through the entire e-learning project management life cycle. If this is your organization's first venture into e-learning course development, the pressure will be on—not just to meet the stated goals of your project but also to prove the value of e-learning within your organization.

Your organization's selection of its first e-learning project is, therefore, one of the most important decisions for creating an e-learning initiative. Your first e-learning project will involve setting up the physical infrastructure for this and subsequent e-learning products. You'll probably be using unfamiliar technology and using untried tools to build and test your e-learning environment. This section may help you avoid some of the pitfalls others have encountered as you launch an e-learning initiative.

7

Project Selection and Project Initiation

Your e-learning program needs to start off on the right foot, and you can do a great deal to ensure the success of a new e-learning initiative by selecting the right kind of project and getting it kicked off with a carefully orchestrated project launch. Picking a project that captures the imagination of your organization and introducing it in a well-run project initiation workshop piques everyone's interest from the moment of its inception.

SELECTING AN E-LEARNING PROJECT

Let's face it: Your first e-learning project shoulders a big responsibility. People are going to be watching to see how effective the product turns out to be, but they are going to be equally curious to see how well you and your team and the others involved in delivering the product work together. E-learning projects require tight timeframes and almost always involve using several very new technologies. They also introduce a whole new array of challenges centered on collaboration and negotiation. You and your team need to work closely with your project sponsors to deliver effective e-learning products. Good communication will be crucial to project success. Therefore, in selecting an e-learning project to use as your first project, try to find one that

- has high visibility and will deliver an e-learning product that is truly needed
- has a true champion—someone who is a steadfast and vocal supporter of the project and has clout and funding—as a project sponsor
- has measurable objectives so that you can easily demonstrate its effectiveness once it is up and running
- deals with a subject area that is not likely to incur too many substantive changes during the development phase

■ relies upon established course development tools, enabling you to defer migration to a new learning management system until after the project is completed

■ has a readily available, committed SME to answer day-to-day questions about content, interface, and other key elements in the e-learning product.

In addition, you want to get agreement about project delivery cycle schedules and make sure all key individuals are available to attend focus group sessions. Don't start the project until everyone understands the new evolutionary development cycle process, the concept of feature trade-offs, and other important adaptive methodology principles. It's not always possible for your first e-learning project to meet all these criteria, but you can increase the probability of success by trying to meet as many of them as possible.

Many different types of projects lend themselves to e-learning solutions. Consider these seven generic types of e-learning projects as you select one to tackle as your first project.

1. E-learning enterprise strategic planning projects are often massive efforts undertaken to produce a comprehensive picture of the current and projected organizational learning needs for an entire corporation or institution. These high-level plans usually focus beyond specific course content to identify skills and knowledge that are the desired output of future e-learning initiatives. Enterprise strategic plans should view organizational learning in its entirety—not just e-learning—without regard for methods of delivery. (Think "nation of communities.")

2. Curriculum definition projects assemble organizational skill and knowledge level requirements into high-level subject areas and begin to enumerate specific courses that would enable e-learning participants to meet these requirements. Curriculums serve as the building blocks for an organization's enterprise e-learning initiative. (Think "community of individuals.")

3. Course development projects identify specific learning content for a course and perform the tasks required to create that content either from scratch or by integration of existing content into the new course. Courses may be used in one or more curriculums. (Think "one individual in a community.")

4. Lesson projects identify a set of topics to be used as part of one or more courses in a curriculum. Lessons may be used in one or more courses. (Think "organs in the individual's body.")

5. Topic projects assemble small units of e-learning content into logical sequences. (Think "molecules.")

6. Content projects produce one specific piece of e-learning content. It is the smallest logic unit of e-learning content. (Think "atoms.")
7. Maintenance and enhancement projects are e-learning projects designed to update or correct existing course content or to add new content to existing e-learning. (Think "hospitals and wellness centers.") Remember, almost every e-learning product will require maintenance or enhancements over time!

If you have a choice, pick a course development project as your first e-learning project. Enterprise strategic plans and curriculum plans for e-learning eventually will be important, but starting out with a proof-of-concept e-learning course development project can help you gain broad support for your e-learning initiative in a relatively short time and at minimal cost. Some organizations have even found success in starting out with a blended approach by first putting course registrations, pretests, and assessment modules online to supplement traditional classroom instruction. In a subsequent project, they develop content to replace the portion taught in the classroom.

DEDICATED TEAMS

It is always preferable to have a dedicated core project team to perform the activities required to complete the project. The more dispersed the team is in terms of focus and geography, the more difficult it is to build a solid collaborative team. Even though the ultimate e-learning product that your team is producing is likely to be one whose learners are widely scattered and probably incapable of meeting face to face, your e-learning development team will be able to get much more accomplished if they are working close together physically. Online collaborative tools are beginning to mitigate some disadvantages of physical separation, but team interaction under one roof remains the most productive environment for teams. Furthermore, large single-room work areas like those used by extreme programming teams offer highly effective models for e-learning project teams.

PURPOSE AND GOALS

The pressure is on you and your team to deliver significant value with your first e-learning project. Your purpose here is not just to provide a valuable e-learning product but also to set the stage for using e-learning in your organization and prove your ability to deliver e-learning in a systematic, efficient manner. Some of the goals of this first project would be to

■ prove that you and your team can deliver an e-learning product on time and within budget

- demonstrate that e-learning course materials and presentation can equal or surpass conventional classroom teaching experiences
- show your ability to create materials that are easily adaptable for future use
- produce e-learning that adds value to your organization
- lay out the infrastructure for continued e-learning development
- reveal an ability to keep business areas engaged and contributing to the e-learning course development effort
- establish a framework for testing and troubleshooting e-learning products
- set up a forum for reporting progress throughout the project.

In other words, your first e-learning project sets the standard for future e-learning development activities. Choose wisely!

THE E-LEARNING PROJECT LIFE CYCLE

As previously outlined, the standard project management life cycle looks like this:

Figure 7-1. The project management life cycle.

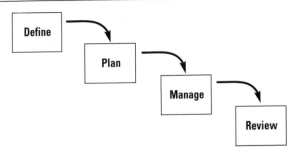

This provides the overview for your e-learning project, but within the overall "Manage" phase of the project, you and your team will follow an adaptive approach that will in effect touch on all four phases of the standard life cycle a number of times.

INITIATING THE PROJECT: SOME CRITICAL SUCCESS FACTORS

The iterative approach has already proven to be a valuable methodology for delivery software products, Websites, standard classroom instruction, and even consumer products. It works well because it guarantees that the key stakeholders in the project will receive tangible proof of the project's progress as it unfolds. It allows for corrections and deviations from the original plan in a manageable way that helps ensure a final product that is what the client wants and needs. If this sounds too good to be true, it's because this new, "agile" approach can work only if *everyone* is aligned with it and understands that project success demands a series of trade-offs.

The project initiation workshop is the first opportunity to bring together the project team and the key stakeholders in the project to create the product vision and to initiate the involved parties in how an iterative, agile approach will work. This workshop requires a number of central elements to be successful:

- The project sponsor should formally endorse the e-learning project, indicate approval of the new approach to managing e-learning projects, require attendance by all personnel who will be working on the project in addition to you and your team, and—if at all possible—be present for at least the opening session of the project launch.
- The project launch agenda should be published well in advance of the session.
- Preliminary orientation materials should be emailed to participants or made available on the Web.
- Tentative dates for review sessions should be put up on the organization's calendar prior to project launch.

You, as project manager, will most likely serve as the facilitator for the launch. If so, identify another individual to act as scribe for the session and decide how the scribe will be recording decisions made and capturing design documents during the launch. If you will not be the facilitator for the launch, plan to meet with both the facilitator and the scribe prior to the launch itself.

Project Launch

The project launch is a facilitated session designed to accomplish important objectives:

- It brings together the project sponsor, the project team, and the remaining cast of characters who will be responsible for the success of the e-learning project.
- It allows everyone involved to create a vision of the product and its most important functions.
- It allows everyone involved to agree on a method of prioritizing features and establishing priorities.
- It allows everyone to agree on the current priority matrix for the project.
- It details the timetables for interim product delivery and interim review sessions.

Roles and Responsibilities

The project launch establishes the roles of all involved. Table 7-1 lists the main players.

Be aware that all these people have "evil twins" lurking inside them. These twins can reveal themselves at the worst possible moment and ruin your project. If the role descriptions in table 7-1 sound too elementary, remember that some of the biggest risks you'll face in managing your e-learning project will come out of people deviating in unexpected ways from their roles. You'll need to keep this list of "unmentionable risks" to yourself, but here are a just a few:

- The project sponsor waffles about priorities and blurts out something like "Well, EVERYTHING is a priority!"
- The project sponsor gives lip service to risk management but won't approve the resources to implement risk management activities in the project.
- You, as project manager, get nervous because the project is running behind schedule and dive in to do other people's work, neglecting your project manager's duties to report progress, manage risks, and negotiate for resources.
- Your project team gets called away to put out other fires in the organization and cannot devote the agreed-upon percentage of effort to the e-learning project.

Table 7-1. Roles and responsibilities of those involved in the e-learning project.

Role	Responsibility
Project Sponsor	The individual responsible for obtaining the funding for the project. A further responsibility involves assisting with decisions regarding changes of scope or priority and approving specific risk-management activities developed to manage the project.
Project Manager	The person who assigns work and prioritizes available resources to produce project deliverables. This person also sees to it that the project sponsor, the business customer, and other stakeholders are aware of the project's progress. The project manager keeps everyone informed of risks threatening the project and steps to be taken to manage those risks.
Project Team	The individuals who will perform the activities required to complete the project. During the completion of these activities, they are to report progress to the project manager and let him or her know of any problems encountered in trying to complete the work.
Business Customer	The person in charge of the business area who will be the beneficiary of the e-learning product when it is implemented. The business customer will see to it that the subject matter experts (SMEs) are available to advise the project team as needed.
SMEs	The people who will help establish the learning objectives for the e-learning product and advise the team regarding content and its appropriateness to those learning objectives. Their availability and participation is critical to the success of the project.

■ The business customer sends conflicting signals to the SMEs about the importance of the e-learning project, giving them other "higher priority" assignments within the department that cut into their availability to you and your team.

■ SMEs have their own agenda about what's important and do not reflect accurately the business needs of the area they represent.

■ SMEs feel threatened by e-learning in general and practice the "sabotage of silence" by withholding important information and dragging their heels when it comes to evaluating and approving project deliverables.

These and other risks you may encounter from "evil twins" make it mandatory for you to spell out role expectations in ways that may help preclude counterproductive behavior.

Creating a Vision for the Product—Revisited

Sometimes you may even want to do an exercise with customers to create a vision for an e-learning solution. Start by using the metaphor of the shrink-wrapped product box. (Think of the format of a typical commercial software product found on the shelves of most computer store chains.) Pretend there already exists an e-learning product with all the features required or desired to solve your e-learning need. In 30 minutes, create a mock-up of the product box, using poster board or flipchart paper. The box front should use "hyped-up" marketing language and graphics to catch the learner's eye and provide immediate appeal. The front of the box should include

- a product name for your e-learning product
- a product logo
- four to seven bullet points indicating major features of the e-learning product.

Then create a mock-up of the package back. It should include

- a 50-word, no-nonsense description of the major functions of the product
- list of 12 to 20 major features of the e-learning product
- three to five learner interface "goodies" (downloadable to a personal digital assistant [PDA], variable bandwidth requirements for home or office use, and so forth).

Finally, create a mock-up of the package side. This is the part that tells you what kind of computer hardware is required to run the product. It should include

- browsers supported
- recommended minimum bandwidth
- any media players required
- any other special requirements to run course from learners' workstations.

This relatively simple exercise can provide a clearer vision of the ultimate e-learning solution in a shorter period of time than using traditional needs analysis alone. The exercise helps make the e-learning product under development more palpable and can, at the very least, provide valuable input for a more detailed needs analysis. Figures 7-2 and 7-3 represent the sides of such a product "box," based on a real e-learning product used by a major corporation (called XYZ).

Figure 7-2. Front of the e-learning product's "box."

Call Center Mentor

The Complete Training Solution for XYZ's Call Center

- **Reduces redundancy**

- **Ensures consistency throughout your organization**

- **Includes Web-based training modules for instant updating**

- **Allows continuous performance monitoring**

- **Reduces training days by 40%**

- **Links to knowledge management and learning management systems**

- **Provides complete learning architecture to meld online learning, classroom training, and knowledge management**

Stating the Objectives of Your E-Learning Product

Based on the results obtained from your needs analysis/product vision activities, you will need to formally state a set of objectives that your e-learning project must meet in order to deliver a successful e-learning solution. Most of these objectives will have shown up as features listed on the "back of the box" during your needs analysis/visioning activities.

Here is a sample list of objectives based on the Call Center Mentor example:

■ Create a Web-based learning environment for Call Center Mentor to partially replace classroom curriculum and coordinate with remaining classroom curriculum.

■ Integrate all relevant modules to the organization's knowledge management system.

Figure 7-3. Back and side of the e-learning product's "box."

Call Center Mentor

The Complete
Training Solution for XYZ's Call Center

Capable of training over 2000 employees in a single year, Call Center Mentor is a complete call center training solution, combining the best elements of classroom instruction and e-Learning. Call Center Mentor is designed to separate systems training, product training, and process training to reduce training time and to ensure that the most important information is introduced first. Call Center Mentor not only reduces training costs and training time but actually increases the total amount of training delivered to each call center staff member.

Here are but a few of Call Center Mentor's features:

1. Web-based modules ensure instant updates and continuous performance monitoring.

2. Tightly integrated learning architecture links directly to the corporate knowledge management system to guarantee consistency of content.

3. Online training modules are closely linked to practice, discussion, and simulations in the classroom.

4. Modules are designed not only to take full advantage of the knowledge management system but also to give the student frequent practice using the knowledge management system so that it becomes an integral part of the daily work routine.

5. Modules for each of the three major product areas are included.

6. Customer service training is fully automated for levels 1, 2, and 3.

7. Core product training is provided for all models of the XYZ product line.

8. Modules start with basic information and build complexity as students master increasingly more challenging content.

9. Participant progress is tracked by location and shift.

10. Areas where participants consistently need more support are flagged.

11. Final practicum leads to interaction with actual customers in a controlled environment.

12. Preliminary tests prove that Call Center Mentor

- reduces costs of delivery

- reduces duration of training for each participant

- enables graduates to reach goals appreciably sooner than previous training methods.

Call Center Mentor

The Complete Training Solution for XYZ's Call Center

SYSTEM REQUIREMENTS

1. XYZ Knowledge Management System

2. Access to XYZ's intranet

3. Microsoft Internet Explorer Version 5.0 and later

- Add online performance support modules.
- Learning modules provide orientation and practice in using XYZ's knowledge management system.
- Learning modules are to cover products from all three of XYZ's major product areas.
- Automate levels 1, 2, and 3 of XYZ's current customer service core training.
- Modules will build on basic curriculum and provide progressively more challenging content.
- All modules must track and report progress at the participant level and report group statistics by location and shift.

Project Objectives Inventory

If your product launch triggers creative thinking among the group members, you may have an embarrassment of riches in terms of potential features and objectives. If this is your first major e-learning effort, you may not have a reliable benchmark for estimating what is possible given the constraints of time and resources. Therefore, it's important to inventory the objectives and features identified and assign priorities.

You will want to meet all the essential objectives for the new e-learning product and introduce the features necessary to meet them as well as other features that add value, enhance ease of use, and increase learner interest and engagement. Classifying objectives and supporting features will allow you to plan for delivery cycles that guarantee that the final product will have optimal immediate and long-range value.

Classify each objective and feature using the following simple scale:

- *Required:* If these features were not included, the e-learning product would be of little or no value. They are the must-have features for the current version of the e-learning product.
- *Highly desirable and will be required for version 2.0:* These are features that can be deferred to the next version of this e-learning product.
- *Highly desirable but not required:* These features would add value to the e-learning product but are not required now or in the foreseeable future.
- *Wish list:* If time allows, these features would be nice to have because they would enhance the e-learning product's attractiveness, add useful but not essential content, or make the product easier to use.
- *Not yet feasible:* These items must be deferred until future technology makes them possible. They would be highly desirable (possibly even required) if the technology to support them were available at a reason-

able cost. At some point in the future, for example, streaming video tutorials might become state-of-the-art for performance support modules on PDAs, but not yet!

This system of classification greatly simplifies planning for current and future e-learning project deliverables. It makes sure no one overlooks an important feature, and it manages expectations about what is possible for the current project.

Critical Success Factors

Those who attend the project launch are certainly the most qualified to enumerate what they expect to see when the project is completed—not only in terms of the final e-learning product itself but also the by-products of the process that created it. They may determine some or all of the following as well as other factors that may be unique to the project:

- All features assigned a priority of "required" will be implemented.
- SMEs are readily available to answer questions throughout the project.
- Turnaround time on documents for review is less than 48 hours.
- All main decision makers attend the cycle review sessions.
- Everyone understands and agrees that any changes to the set of features will require that the project be reestimated and that such changes will result in forgoing a feature, adding additional resources, or extending the final delivery date.
- Stakeholders will receive regular progress reports.
- SMEs will work closely with the development team to review and test e-learning modules throughout each development cycle before each cycle review session.
- The project team and the target business area will work together and produce criteria for product evaluation at each of four levels of evaluation (Horton, 2001b).

EVOLUTIONARY CYCLE PLANNING

Once the project launch session is complete, you and your team have the necessary information to create a plan for delivering the e-learning product through a series of time-boxed cycles, each culminating in an interim review session to demonstrate the functionality of the product and to make any adjustments to the feature list as required, keeping in mind the priority matrix established regarding time/cost/scope.

Each interim review session will focus on a working version of the e-learning product in its current incarnation and will be able to show off the features that have been implemented up to the present time. The final interim review session will prove the viability of the completed product. The art and science of cycle planning involves implementing required features in a sequence that will allow you and your team to test and demonstrate them at each interim review session and respond to requested changes without the necessity of substantial rework or abandonment of features.

During project initiation, you identified required features and features that were desirable but deferrable. Your cycle plan should guarantee delivery of all required features and as many desirable features as possible within the time and resource constraints of the project.

PICKING THE RIGHT THINGS TO MEASURE

In examining critical success factors, make sure you are picking the things that really matter for your organization. And, remember that really important factors, such as overall business productivity and other long-term benefits of e-learning, may be the hardest to prove (or at least will take the longest to prove). It's fine to include those measurements and to try to capture information that may indicate that e-learning is making a long-term difference. Nonetheless, pick a few things that will show up early enough to give immediate momentum to your e-learning initiative (for example, response evaluations from e-learning courses compared with those from classroom instruction for the same course content or cost savings to provide instruction to 500 employees compared with the costs of bringing people to the training center). These kinds of measurements can build support for e-learning. Keep honing your measurement criteria with each project, but try to standardize the process as much as possible.

PROJECT ESTIMATING

One thing is certain: Your first project task estimates will tend to be "ball park" estimates unless you already have a group of people in your organization who have completed some e-learning projects. You may get some suggestions from other organizations who have completed e-learning projects, but your own situation—particularly at the time you are embarking on your first e-learning project—may be sufficiently unique to cast doubt on the accuracy of another organization's project estimates.

Well, then, it sounds hopeless! Not really. Part of the idea behind cycle planning is to test your ability to come up with viable activity estimates. Don't break down the structure too far; keep activities chunked to, say, the hypertext mark-up language (HTML) page level. The next level up might be the lesson level, with its additional overhead and navigation requirements. You may, for example, determine that an average HTML page takes 2 hours to design and test. To create a lesson with 12 pages and navigation would take 12 × 2 hours plus a substantial margin (perhaps 20 percent) for navigation and other requirements. Another 10 percent would be required for testing of links. Finally, round all estimates up before entering them. (Decimal places in project estimates imply a degree of predictive powers that most mortals lack.) Thus, a 12-page lesson might yield an estimate of 32 hours:

Develop HTML course pages	12 × 2 hours	24.0 hours
Add-on for navigation	+ 20%	4.8 hours
Add-on for testing	+ 10%	2.4 hours
Total estimated time		31.2 hours = 32.0 hours

Chapter 10 provides you a complete project estimating example.

YOUR TURN

Go over the seven kinds of e-learning projects listed earlier in this chapter, and in worksheet 7-1 give examples of projects your own organization might undertake in the future.

Worksheet 7-1. Potential projects by level of complexity.

1. E-Learning Enterprise Strategic Planning Projects

What are some of the broad knowledge areas that your organization's strategic plan might address?

What large business goals would those knowledge areas support?

How?

2. Curriculum Definition Projects

Identify one specific subject area that your organization would develop a curriculum for.

Who would be your internal SMEs to determine the skill sets required?

Where might you go outside your organization for additional help?

What kinds of reports would you produce for this project? Who would receive these reports?

What are some risks that might be unique to this kind of project?

3. Course Development Projects

For the curriculum you identified above, think of a specific course that would likely be included in that curriculum. What would that course be?

Could it be used in any other curriculums for your organization?

Do you know of any potential partners outside the walls of your organization with whom you might collaborate to produce this course as an e-learning course?

4. Lesson Projects

Name a specific lesson for the course you identified in item 3.

List some topics that would probably be part of that lesson:

Worksheet 7-1. Potential projects by level of complexity (continued).

5. Topic Projects

Might any of the topics named in item 4 be included in some other course offered in your organization? If so, what additional steps should you take to ensure ease of reuse and identification?

Should you consider taking such steps for all lesson topics? Why or why not?

6. Content Projects

Think of one specific piece of content (for example, an important fact about your organization) that would be likely to be used in many different e-learning courses covering a multitude of subjects.

Do you think there will many more of these "knowledge nuggets" that you'll want to make available to other e-learning course developers within your organization?

If so, how should you go about organizing these pieces of content?

What will happen when a fact or statistic changes?

7. Maintenance and Enhancement Projects

How much e-learning content (courses, lessons, topics, content modules) will require updating at least once a year? More often? Less often? What will never require updates?

As your e-learning effort expands over time, what will happen to your maintenance/enhancement workload? Do all stakeholders in your organization understand this?

If not, how can you as an e-learning project manager prepare them for future needs?

8

Parallel Universes: Building the Infrastructure

You may be fortunate enough never to have to worry about the physical hardware components of e-learning, but it is more likely that you will have a number of concerns about the infrastructure that supports your e-learning environment. No matter how well you've designed your e-learning course product, e-learners need to have computers that are fast enough to run the course materials, and they must have stable Internet connections linked to reliable e-learning Web servers to enable them to pursue their e-learning studies. As an e-learning course developer, your success depends on designing and implementing courses that can run in a variety of settings, using a number of standard Web browsers, and using plug-ins that are easily available to your e-learning audience.

DUE TO TECHNICAL DIFFICULTIES, %#&*@$!

So what could possibly go wrong? Read on:

- *Bugs in the course material pages themselves:* Even with rigorous testing you may have errors in course pages or links that can create nightmares for e-learners. One of the big temptations in trying to keep e-learning projects on schedule is to skimp on testing time. Don't yield to this temptation; the consequences are too great.
- *Incompatibilities with certain Web browsers:* You may decide to require only two or three Web browsers and specify minimum version levels. Your development and test plans need to take into account the time required to test on all "authorized" browsers.
- *Media players and other plug-ins not available on all e-learner workstations:* Have these components readily available as part of your course materials, but realize that setting up these components adds to the workload for your project.

■ *E-learning materials run very slowly on older workstations or workstations with insufficient memory:* Too often the development team works with cutting-edge workstations, forgetting that the end users of their product have much less capable configurations. Make sure tests are performed on slower stations. Consider developing alternative media for low-end configurations. Again, this consideration adds to your project schedule!

The list goes on. For each project, consider specific kinds of technical threats. These certainly are major parts of your project's risk assessment. Many concerns about infrastructure and workstation capabilities translate into your need to build in components to enable e-learners with less computer power or with slower Internet connections to participate without substantial loss of content.

LEARNING CONTENT MANAGEMENT SYSTEMS

The core of a successful e-learning initiative is its learning content management system (LCMS), a centralized repository for your e-learning content and the means to organize, update, and distribute e-learning to your e-learning audience. Your decision to build or buy an LCMS depends on just how much e-learning content you plan to develop, how many authors and developers will be involved, how widely distributed your team members are, how much money you have to spend initially, and other factors unique to your organization. Whatever you decide, make sure you have the functions listed in table 8-1 covered within your organization—with or without the help of a dedicated tool.

If you already have an LCMS in place and are familiar with how to use it, you will have the advantage of templates and established procedures to simplify the production of your final e-learning product. It will also save you the steps necessary to perform the LCMS-type functions outlined in the table. Nevertheless, make sure your project plan includes activities to

■ set up user accounts and permissions for your e-learning project team
■ add metadata information for e-learning content as you create it
■ create distribution procedure entries
■ review content for compliance with standards.

If you are building your own LCMS, trying to cover LCMS-type functions on your own, or are learning how to use a newly acquired LCMS, your project needs to take into account

■ the learning curve for users of the new LCMS, including training and orientation of team members
■ definitions of your tagging elements for metadata
■ forms and templates for learning objects

Table 8-1. What your LCMS (or you) must accomplish.

LCMS Function	What You Need to Have Covered
Serve as a repository	Establish a centralized location where all e-learning content, cataloging information, and implementation and distribution procedures can be stored, accessed, and updated by e-learning developers.
Control creation, access, reuse, and sharing of e-learning content	Set up check-in/check-out procedures to help developers create and share common elements, templates, style sheets, learning modules, graphic elements, etc.
Provide security	Establish security to control such functions as updating or distribution of e-learning materials to production.
Assist with defining and maintaining learning objects for reuse	Keep your content elements modular so that they can be used in more than one e-learning product. Formalizing this process into "learning objects" helps ensure consistency and ease of updating elements when they occur in multiple e-learning courses.
Provide metadata information about e-learning elements	Develop a system of tagging all e-learning elements that provides documentation about author, update history, courses used, subject area, and any other data that would be searchable by your course developers (and often by your e-learners themselves) if they are looking for a particular kind of content.
Automate procedures for assembling and distributing e-learning content	Your ability to provide customized e-learning content for learners means that eventually there will simply be too many "versions" of a course. See to it that you have created and catalogued procedures that can be followed—and eventually automated—to manage the complexity of e-learning distribution as your e-learning curriculum grows.
Maintain update schedules for e-learning	Make sure you have a centralized calendar for posting upcoming expiration dates for e-learning content with limited shelf life.
Conform to accepted e-learning standards	Your purchased or home-grown LCMS needs to conform to current e-learning standards. As your e-learning program expands and LCMSs mature, having your repository's content comply with an existing standard will make moving to the next one much, much simpler.

- meetings with IT department to set up distribution procedures, staging areas, and so forth.
- meetings with other e-learning project managers to reach agreement on name conventions, tagging rules, and so forth.

Never assume that purchasing an LCMS is the answer to all your e-learning needs. An LCMS can help you manage your organization's e-learning content and facilitate the management of e-learning projects, but you can be sure that you'll still have numerous LCMS administrative activities as part of every e-learning project. Don't overlook these activities in creating your e-learning project plans.

STANDARDS? WHO NEEDS 'EM?

Standards are moving targets right now. Eventually, the world may decide on a single standard that everyone is happy with. In the meantime, you'll want to comply with one of the currently accepted e-learning standards if you have a choice in selecting a tool or in building your own e-learning objects. If you follow a current standard, future tools will more than likely provide you a migration path to the "final standard" if one comes along. Standards compliance and quality reviews around standards will add activities to your project plan.

AUTHOR, BEWARE!

Don't let a flashy demonstration hoodwink you into believing that a piece of course development software is going to answer all your problems. Like LCMSs, these products are evolving. You are probably going to use one of these tools, and it will simplify many tasks as you and your team develop your e-learning product. Leave room in your project plan for learning how to use the tool—plenty of room if it's a new tool or new version of an existing tool. Software manufacturers also balance freedom-from-defects with time-to-market as they introduce new tools. With new tools or new versions of existing tools, add on an extra 10 or 20 percent duration to every activity using the tool for relearning and recovery time. If the product is brand new to you and your organization, include training time. Try not to reinvent the wheel; use existing tools, especially if your organization already has other e-learning projects that rely on them.

BUILD VERSUS BUY

You'll need to consider the advantages of purchasing not only an LCMS and authoring tools but also learning content itself. The availability of prewritten e-learning courses, modules, and templates increases daily. Costs and quality vary widely, and there isn't always a direct correlation between cost and quality. Your e-learning project plan may want to include evaluation of available solutions produced by outside firms.

WHO CAN HELP?

Your membership in organizations like ASTD can bring you into contact with other e-learning project managers who are trying to launch similar e-learning initiatives in their organizations or already have success stories (or horror stories) to share about their experiences with LCMSs, authoring tools, and pre-built e-learning products. You may also find it helpful to develop alliances to share some of your own e-learning products, tools, or templates you've developed. Network as much as you can before you start your e-learning project and throughout the project to develop a group of colleagues to act as your "third eye" and help guide your decision making.

Of course, there are scores of qualified consultants who could help; and you can consider using paid coaches to get you started with your e-learning initiative. The same colleagues who will be your sources for e-learning advice can also offer recommendations about finding consulting assistance. Their endorsements should count more than glossy brochures from the consulting firms themselves.

YOUR TURN

Pick three popular Websites and two sites that offer e-learning content. If your company has a high-speed T-1 line, use it for each of the five sites. Jot down how long each activity takes. If you or a friend has a cable modem connection, try those same activities from a computer using a cable modem. Likewise, try these same activities from a digital subscriber line (DSL) hookup. Finally, try them from a standard 56-K dial-up connection. Log the respective times on worksheet 8-1.

Worksheet 8-1. Performance comparisons.

Site	T-1 Time	Cable Time	DSL Time	56-K Time

Based on your findings, answer the questions posed in worksheet 8-2.

Worksheet 8-2. Connectivity and your e-learning projects.

What do these time comparisons tell you about planning your e-learning course?

Do you have any members of your project team working from home offices? If so, should you consider obtaining high-speed connections for them for the period they are working on your project?

What additional testing procedures should you consider adding to avoid bandwidth problems once your e-learning course is deployed?

Part 3
Getting Your E-Learning Project Off the Ground

Earlier you learned about the components of the project definition, saw how project deliverables mapped into activities dedicated to producing those deliverables, examined the role of anticipating and dealing with risk and changes to the project during the management phase, and read how the review process not only helped capture lessons learned at the end of the project but also could be used to improve your project work during the project as well.

Now you're ready to start a real e-learning project. You'll apply all the principles described thus far to a collaborative, product-focused development effort that includes your team, content SMEs, your organization's IT department, and a sample of your intended learning audience. You'll learn how focus groups can provide feedback and gauge progress as you and your team provide incremental delivery of the e-learning product. Your final product and the experiences that went into producing it will become the springboard for subsequent e-learning projects as you begin to develop a climate for continuous improvement in your e-learning program.

9

Preparing to Launch Your E-Learning Project

Creating an e-learning project is a collaborative venture. You and your project team need to structure the project in such a way that the customer and all those involved in the project remain committed from the very inception of the project through its completion and deployment within the organization. Building an environment that facilitates this kind of interaction requires a new approach—one that provides an opportunity to demonstrate progress, makes certain that lines of communication remain open, and manages risks and changes throughout the life of the project.

Using Focus Groups

The focus group is a facilitated session designed to obtain valuable information about a proposed product or service. The focus group is a relatively quick, inexpensive method of gathering requirements for a final product, especially when coupled with prior research into overall business goals and performance objectives for e-learning participants. Traditional learning need assessments can provide invaluable inputs into the preliminary focus group and help ensure that the focus group results lead to a successful e-learning product.

Why Focus Groups?

Focus groups offer several important benefits for project-managing e-learning:

- Focus groups allow you to accomplish a great deal in a compressed time-frame. Bringing everyone together guarantees that ideas get shared and that important points are brought up for decision.
- Focus groups provide fixed time points for project milestones. The project initiation focus group sets the stage for upcoming interim focus groups. Your project, therefore, has not one "drop dead" deadline at the

end but rather a series of deadlines designed to demonstrate progress and reach decisions about the deliverables for the upcoming focus group sessions.

■ Focus groups keep stakeholders actively participating throughout the project. Too often in projects, the initial momentum falls off after project launch. Well-managed focus groups provide a method of building and sustaining support for the project for all stakeholders.

■ Focus groups make customers and stakeholders active participants in the design process. At first, the design is more concept than working model, although you may sometimes have interface prototypes from other completed e-learning products to demonstrate even at the project initiation focus group. Once the project is under way, however, focus group reviews should center on the current working version of the new e-learning product.

RECRUITING CUSTOMERS

Focus group customers should include SMEs, business representatives from the area requesting the e-learning product, and a small but representative section of individuals who would be e-learners using the product. The role of the business representative is to ensure that the content matches the learning objectives spelled out in the project definition. The e-learners provide feedback about the effectiveness of the product in engaging learners and making the e-learning experience a positive one. Generally both groups interact with a facilitator (sometimes the project manager but, better still, a neutral party) and a scribe (usually a member of the project team or the project manager) to evaluate the proposed product, spot areas that need improvement or correction, and determine priorities for the features to be included in the product.

FOCUS GROUP SCENARIOS

Within a given e-learning project, three basic types of focus groups are used:

1. *Project initiation focus groups:* These are designed to formulate the vision for the product, determine the major functionality to be included, identify desirable learning delivery methods, and assign priorities to these functions and methods. The input of this session is the project definition. The output is a prioritized function and feature set, along with validated scope documents, a risk control plan, and a communications plan.

2. *Interim focus groups:* These are designed to be forums for demonstrating the e-learning product, testing its learning worthiness, and revisiting priorities for the remainder of the project. The input for this session is the latest version of the delivery cycle plan. Output is approvals of work

to date, requests for rework, and reprioritization of remaining items scheduled for delivery.

3. *Project acceptance focus group:* This group is designed to garner final acceptance of the completed project, conduct a formal review process, and collect best practices and recommendations for future projects. Inputs are a final cycle delivery plan, project definition, progress reports, and relevant scope and risk management documentation. Output is an approved acceptance document, signed review documents, and best practices recommendations.

ANALYZING CHANGING REQUIREMENTS

It's really true that the focus group always does, in fact, clear up a blurry picture of the project and brings it into a sharp, renewed focus. The project initiation workshop turns abstract requirements into a picture of what the product might look like. The interim focus groups take the current product and help steer it in a new or revised direction, thus retouching the original picture. The project acceptance focus group puts a seal of approval on the product and places it in the perspective of the overall e-learning initiative for your organization.

PROTOTYPING VERSUS FOCUS GROUPS

Lest there be any doubt, please remember that focus groups will be reviewing a real, working e-learning product rather than throwaway prototypes. Delivery cycles are simply too short to waste time creating models that have no use. The project initiation workshop is perhaps the only exception to this rule. At that early stage, objectives should be translated into features and general descriptions of the types of delivery methods and interfaces to be used.

Prototypes at this stage may be storyboards, drawings, and perhaps a few prefabricated interface controls used for demonstration purposes. Once the project initiation workshop is completed, any development work should operate under the assumption that the deliverable being produced will be part of the final e-learning product. Obviously, when rework is truly necessary, a certain—and, it is hoped, small—percentage of the deliverables will have to be replaced or significantly revised. Most work should produce "keepers."

CUSTOMER FOCUS GROUP BENEFITS

Once you've established the focus group as the primary means of demonstrating project progress, revisiting priorities, and keeping communications channels open, you are well on your way to keeping customers involved and contributing to your e-learning effort. What's more, they'll become e-learning boosters as they realize that their input has value and gets results!

Special Case for Project Initiation Workshops

You may determine that there is an e-learning product already on hand or existing at another organization that seems to come close to meeting the objectives stated in the project definition. You might want to use the existing product as a prototype for the e-learning product you are defining. To do this, you'd follow these steps:

1. Match the features of the existing product to corresponding project objectives.
2. Demonstrate these features as part of the project initiation workshop.
3. Create a matrix of objectives, features that match, and gaps where no feature exists to fulfill the objective.
4. Indicate for each objective what features would need to be added, which features would be removed, and which features would need to be changed significantly.

You may or may not have the ability to adapt the existing product, but you've used it as a powerful tool to clarify the vision of your final product for your customer and your project team.

YOUR TURN

Think of a likely e-learning project for your organization and see if you can come up with your focus group "guest list" on worksheet 9-1. Indicate each participant's name and position, role in the project, strengths (special value or contribution they can bring to the group), and cautions associated with that individual or role. Cautions can stem from many causes, ranging from technophobia to a lack of time for sessions.

Worksheet 9-1. E-learning focus group "guest list."

Description of Project:

Likely duration of such a project:

Number of delivery cycles:

Invitee Name and Position	Focus Group Role	Strengths	Cautions

10

Launching and Managing the Project

The primary deliverables emanating from the project initiation focus group included an overall e-learning product vision—a list of the major functions the e-learning product would perform—linked to specific learning objectives, desired methods for content delivery, and priorities for these functions and content delivery methods. What's more, you have now established a preliminary timetable for interim and final focus group sessions and have agreement about how you and your project team will work with the e-learning SMEs to create the product. Now the work begins!

In this chapter, you will have a chance to follow along in the planning of an e-learning course using templates to help with estimating and tracking your project. You will see examples of how to think through an e-learning project, produce a statement of work, plan iterative delivery cycles, determine methods for managing risks, and create the framework for delivering your e-learning product. You will see how to estimate resource and effort requirements to e-learning course development, including testing and demonstrating your evolving product to your customers. By the end of the chapter you will have a good idea of what goes into project planning and scheduling for e-learning course development.

NOW WHAT?

You have most of the information required to plan and deliver the e-learning product. The preliminary timeframe is set. At this point, however, you and your team need to evaluate the proposed schedule in terms of numbers of features to be delivered, resources available (including reusable e-learning objects and templates built from previous projects), and the complexity of the features to be delivered. If time is the main constraint, you may need to renegotiate to reduce the number of features to be produced or to increase the total resources dedicated to the project once you've estimated the effort required to produce the e-learning product as it was defined during the project initiation focus group.

The days following the project initiation focus group session are crucial to the creation of a successful project delivery plan and the ultimate success of your project.

THE E-LEARNING PROJECT STATEMENT OF WORK

If you are creating the e-learning product for a customer outside the organization, you need to perform a series of project management tasks—known as the statement of work (SOW)—to turn the preliminary delivery cycle plan into a solid e-learning project plan. Your plan, or SOW, should address the following:

- e-learning product intent and overall design considerations
- a breakdown of specific deliverables for each feature and function
- overall project management considerations.

The following sections address each of these SOW components in some detail.

E-Learning Product Intent and Overall Design Considerations

Restate Key Points of Project Instructional Design. Who is the primary e-learning audience? What are the stated learning objectives? What are the methods of assessing learner progress and competencies during and after participation in the e-learning course?

Context Diagram for the E-Learning Product. This graphic provides an "aerial view" of the product, as well as the entities and systems that interact with it. Who or what "feeds" the product, and what types of information (in addition to content pages) are fed to stakeholders and other systems?

Internal Training Versus External Marketing. Clarifying the audience helps clarify the ultimate performance objectives for learners. That is, does the e-learning product intend to improve specific on-the-job skills or is its primary purpose to cultivate customer loyalty or help the customer make a purchasing or enrollment decision?

IT Infrastructure Requirements. Will your internal IT department host the e-learning product on existing servers, acquire additional servers for hosting, or assist you in securing the services of an outside Internet service provider (ISP) or application service provider (ASP)?

Performance Criteria. How many learners do you anticipate will be accessing the Website? Are you training a few dozen employees at a time, or are you expecting hundreds or thousands of learners to access the course?

Projected Hardware and Bandwidth Capability of Learners. Are learners *always* going to be participating in the e-learning at work with high-speed connections, or will they often be using dial-up connections from home or on the road as well?

Choice of Authoring Tools. Within the organization, are other e-learning products in place that used one of the currently available authoring tools? How familiar is the project team with this product? If the e-learning product will be developed using a new authoring tool, what are the specific operating system requirements and database software for the hosting server? Are these compliant with your IT department's specifications?

Web Browser Compatibility Requirements. Is it necessary to accommodate more than one browser or to be backward compatible to several previous versions of a specific browser? If so, you place additional burdens on the developers and testers of the e-learning product. If possible, limit the product to a single version of a single browser, although this situation is probably true only for organizations producing in-house e-learning.

Bookmarking, Scoring, and Other Tracking Requirements. Are these features necessities or are they merely attractive conveniences? Remember, bookmarking, scoring, and tracking can add considerable additional development work for your project.

LMS Requirements. Does your company already have a systemwide learning management system (LMS) that requires AICC (Airline Industry CBT Committee) or SCORM (Shareable Content Object Reference Model) compliance to bookmark and track user scores? If you have not already purchased an LMS, should you consider renting (paying per user) LMS services from an ASP to track, score, and host? If AICC or SCORM compatibility is a requirement, have you identified which elements of the e-learning product will need to be tested for compliance? Demonstrating compliance may involve a significant investment of team effort and should focus on elements that are relevant and critical to your e-learning product. What is your testing plan?

Accessibility Requirements. Will your e-learning product have to be accessible to the disabled? Will the project therefore need to incorporate special software or audio for every page of e-learning content?

Requirements for Ongoing Support. After implementation of the e-learning product, who will be responsible for keeping content up to date? What documentation is required for IT? What procedures need to be established for changing content and assessment modules of the e-learning product? Who sets up users and passwords for the e-learning course? What steps will be required to meet your IT department's security requirements?

Style Guide and Template "Look" and "Feel." Who will provide storyboards to illustrate the look and feel of the graphics for your e-learning product? Are there specific branding requirements? If so, who will create font and color scheme specifications and provide sample menu and content pages?

Breakdown of Specific Deliverables for Each Feature and Function

Number of Lesson Modules, Templates, and HTML Pages Required. The number of lesson modules influences the overall structure for the e-learning product and for your iterative delivery cycles. You will also have to determine the number of templates that can be used from previous e-learning products and how many will have to be created. You may also find for many of your e-learning projects that the HTML page can serve as a useful unit for estimating effort. Nevertheless, you may wish to classify pages into a few categories based on the degree of complexity of the page (number of graphical or media objects, pages that trigger database queries, and so forth). Keep the number of categories small, though. At this point you are trying to establish estimation benchmarks—not just for your current e-learning project but for subsequent e-learning efforts as well.

Media Content. Estimate the typical number of media elements to be included on each category of page. Also determine the types of media to be included on each page (text, graphics, interactive sequences, audio, and video).

High-Level Product Testing Scripts. Test planning needs to start from the moment you begin to design your e-learning product. Determine the kinds of tests—navigation, external links, database queries, user volume, and so forth—that will need to be conducted before you publish your e-learning product.

Navigation Rules. The complexity of these rules has a considerable effect on the amount of effort required to produce the e-learning product. Webpage navigation invoked by clicking through standard page structures is straightforward. More complex rules based on learner responses is slightly more complicated. Rules that require maintenance of learner profiles heap additional work on the e-learning course developer.

Overall Project Management Considerations

Roles and Responsibilities. Here you reiterate who will be involved in the production of the e-learning product, who will approve the product's readiness for implementation, who will approve changes to specifications and resource requirements, and who must be included in status reports for the project. Furthermore, here is where you state your expectations about availability of staffing resources, commitment for participation in subsequent cycle reviews, and so forth.

Risk Management. Based on the risks identified in your original project definition and on any new risks uncovered in the project initiation focus group, determine which risks require preventive action, steps to mitigate their impact if they occur, and any additional contingency measures to prepare for deployment should the risk occur. These preventive and contingency activities add to the overall effort for the project.

Relative Priorities of Time, Cost, Quality/Scope. Once again, revisit the priority matrix. If time is your main constraint, then establishing your delivery cycles is fairly simple. If cost or quality/scope are the highest priorities, you may need to juggle the delivery cycles based on the requirements, resource availability, cost constraints, and other considerations.

Number of Delivery Cycles. Rule of thumb: For any project with a delivery date 3 to 6 months from project launch, plan for two or three interim cycle reviews and a final cycle review. For projects with more distant completion dates, consider interim cycle reviews every 6 to 8 weeks. (It is rare for an e-learning project to have that kind of lead time.)

ESTIMATING RESOURCE/EFFORT REQUIREMENTS

The e-learning project SOW gives you a solid basis for estimating the total resource and effort requirements for your e-learning project. You've specified the content components of your e-learning product, the hardware and software requirements for developing the product and for supporting it after implementation. You've determined the project reporting requirements and appropriate levels of reporting detail for project team members, clients, the project sponsor, and other stakeholders. You've identified the risks that require preventative steps or steps to reduce impact. You've established responsibilities for certain types of tasks for your project. You also have the required supportive project management tasks described in chapter 4. Follow these 15 steps to complete the first pass at your estimate:

1. *Framework:* Determine the tasks required to create the high-level course framework based on the number of lesson modules required and estimate the effort for each task.

2. *Creation of new templates:* Estimate the effort required to create any new templates for the course.

3. *Adaptation of existing templates:* Estimate the effort required to adapt any existing templates for the course.

4. *Media and interactive elements:* Estimate the effort required to create each media element type. For instance, a text or Adobe Photoshop element may require half an hour, but a 45-second video or Macromedia Flash or Shockwave element may require a day or longer to create. Audio and video elements may entail extensive outsourcing, taking on the dimensions of a subproject within a larger e-learning project.

5. *Page-level test cases and test scripts:* Estimate the effort required to create test cases and test scripts for each page type. The testing script for pages with database queries, for instance, calls for a more exhaustive set of cases than a simple presentation page.

6. *Navigation rule test cases and test scripts:* Estimate the effort required to create test cases and test scripts to test complex navigation rules.

7. *Tests for bookmarking:* Estimate the effort required to create test cases and scripts for bookmarking, if it is required.

8. *Page-level testing:* Estimate the effort to run the testing scripts from steps 5 through 7. (For now, your estimates should address the effort required to run the tests using a single browser. Later, you'll adjust testing estimates by a factor based on the number of browsers your e-learning product has to support.)

9. *Capacity (stress) testing:* Estimate the effort to test the infrastructure's learner-volume capacity. Setting up a test environment can be costly. Look into this as early as possible if you expect many learners to be using your e-learning product at the same time.

10. *Standards compliance:* Identify activities and estimate effort required to conform to AICC/SCORM standards.

11. *Risk management:* For each risk management item that requires action, break it down into tasks and estimate the effort required for each task.

12. *Documentation and support activities:* Estimate the activities and related effort needed to meet support and internal documentation requirements.

13. *Weekly reporting and ongoing project management tasks:* If possible estimate the effort required *each week* for these activities.

14. *Focus group activities:* Estimate the activities and associated effort for preparation of agendas, meeting room preparation, report documents, and any other activities that relate to focus group review sessions. Oh, and

don't forget the time spent in the focus group session itself! It may sound strange, but project managers have, on occasion, failed to factor in the time spent in the group session itself. Considering the number of players involved in a session, this can be a serious oversight!

15. *Cycle planning activities:* This first planning effort, described here, is the most time-consuming part of the iterative process and one of the most valuable. After each interim focus group session, you will have to revise the plan for the remainder of the project. After each interim focus group session, estimate at least a full day to work with your team to plan and publish the revised plan for the remaining cycles.

PLANNING THE DELIVERY CYCLES

Delivery cycles allow you to create an e-learning product that truly meets your customer's wants and needs. The project initiation focus group served as the forum for collaborative envisioning of the final product. That vision was based on the best information available about the e-learning product's objectives and how you and the customer envisioned the product at the time. But, as anyone ever involved in a development project can tell you, people's foresight is imperfect. The customer may have overlooked an important point, or you and your team may have misunderstood a requirement.

Prototyping is the first line of defense against such misunderstandings. But throw-away prototypes are wasteful. You and your customer want to spend as much time and effort as possible producing a real, working e-learning product. This is where delivery cycles come in.

Obviously, you'll be working frequently with members of the customer and stakeholder community in developing your e-learning course, but at a few points along the way it is important to bring *everyone* together, give a thorough presentation of the portions of the e-learning product developed to date, and revise or reconfirm plans for the remaining development activities. Delivery cycles formalize this practice.

SAMPLE PROJECT TO ILLUSTRATE CYCLE PLANNING

Let's assume you are building a 10-lesson e-learning course. After analyzing the project definition coming out of the preliminary focus group session, you have derived estimates for delivering the e-learning course components using a project team of five (including yourself) over a 13-week period. You hold interim focus group sessions at the end of the fourth and eighth weeks and the project acceptance focus group session in the 13th week. Figure 10-1 illustrates the delivery cycle process.

Figure 10-1. Sample iterative e-learning project.

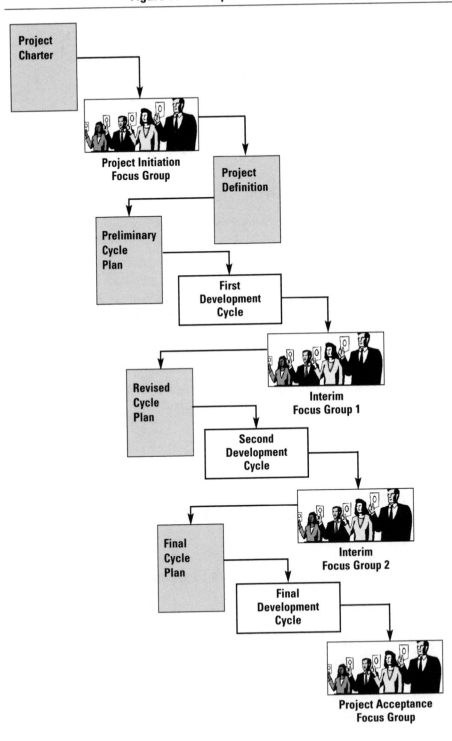

Project Charter

Project Initiation Focus Group

Project Definition

Preliminary Cycle Plan

First Development Cycle

Interim Focus Group 1

Revised Cycle Plan

Second Development Cycle

Interim Focus Group 2

Final Cycle Plan

Final Development Cycle

Project Acceptance Focus Group

Developing an Architectural Plan for the Sample Project

If this is your first e-learning project, getting the overall architecture of the e-learning course and its components estimated will seem a formidable task. However, if you break it into logical parts, it will not only simplify the process but also give you much greater control over your e-learning project. It will also provide the basis for continuous refinement of how you estimate projects in the future.

Develop estimating guidelines for using existing course page templates (style sheets) and for creating any new template that may be required. (If this is your first e-learning project, of course, all the templates will be new. This means additional effort for each page using a new template.) For the current example, assume you will be using preexisting page templates most of the time. However, you will need to develop a few new templates as well. Before you start to estimate the actual project, try to classify your existing page templates into categories based on their complexity as shown in table 10-1. (This example simply calls each template category type 1, type 2, and so forth.)

Estimate Effort for Creating New Templates

Of course, for your first e-learning projects, almost all the templates will be brand new, requiring additional effort on your part. If, however, you develop each template with the idea of reusing it, your subsequent projects will take less effort. You can estimate the amount of time needed to create a new template as shown in table 10-2.

Next, determine how many new page template designs will be needed for your e-learning project. Then, multiply the number of new page templates by the estimated effort to obtain the estimated effort for creating all the new templates in your project. The sample project requires the design of a few new page templates as shown in table 10-3.

Estimate Time for Administrative Activities and Focus Groups

Table 10-4 indicates how to estimate hours for focus group activities and project management administration activities for the sample project.

Inventory Pages for the Lesson

You've already estimated the effort to add content to each type of page. Therefore, you will be able to calculate the base effort for creating content for

Table 10-1. Templates classified by typical types and numbers of elements per page.

Templates Classified by Typical Types and Numbers of Elements per Page

Template Type	Text Elements	Image Elements	Audio Media Elements	Interactive Elements	Database Queries
Type 1	1	4	0	0	0
Type 2	1	4	1	0	0
Type 3	1	4	1	0	1
Type 4	1	4	1	1	1
Assessment	1	4	0	0	20

Type of Element	Effort Hours
Text	0.5
Image	0.5
Audio	2.0
Interactive	8.0
Database	0.5

Estimated effort (in hours) for adding one element of content to a given page

Calculation of Effort to Add Content for All Elements on a Given Page

Template Type	Text Elements	Image Elements	Audio Media Elements	Video Elements	Database Queries	Total Effort
Type 1	0.5	2	0	0	0	2.5
Type 2	0.5	2	2	0	0	4.5
Type 3	0.5	2	2	0	0.5	5.0
Type 4	0.5	2	2	8	0.5	13.0
Assessment	0.5	2	0	0	10	12.5

Table 10-2. Estimating effort necessary to create new templates.

New Template Creation	Effort Hours
Type 1	2
Type 2	3
Type 3	3
Type 4	4
Assessment	6

Estimated effort (in hours) to create new template shells

Table 10-3. Estimate the effort required to produce new templates for the project.

New Template for Project	Effort Hours
Type 1	4 pages $\times$ 2 = 8
Type 2	3 pages $\times$ 3 = 9
Type 3	2 pages $\times$ 3 = 6
Type 4	2 pages $\times$ 4 = 8
Assessment	0 pages $\times$ 6 = 0
Total effort:	**31**

your course once you know how many pages of each template type you will need to produce. You can inventory the pages for the sample project using table 10-5.

Determine the Total Effort for the Course

Now, calculate the production effort per lesson and for the course by multiplying the number of pages by the estimated effort for each page type. Table 10-6 shows how these calculations would look for the sample project.

Develop basic estimating guidelines for proofing and testing the pages (table 10-7). Remember, you'll be refining these estimates as you and your organization gain experience in delivering e-learning products.

You now can calculate the estimated testing effort for each lesson and for the entire course by multiplying the number of pages by the estimated effort to test each page type. Table 10-8 represents these calculations for the sample e-learning project.

Table 10-4. Estimating level of effort for administration and focus group meetings.

Administration and Focus Group Support Activities	Base Effort	Role(s)	Base Effort in Hours	Units	Total Hours in Project
Weekly project management re: focus groups	4 hours/week	Project manager	6	13	78
Preparation for focus groups	2 days per session	Project manager and team	42	3	126
Preparation and distribution of focus group outcomes	1 day per session	Project manager and team member serving as scribe	12	3	36
Focus group meetings	1 day per session	Project manager and team	24	3	72
Administrative activities (reviewing progress, risk management, project team support, etc.)	35% add-on to all task estimates	Project manager and team	210	1	210
				Total:	522

Team size (including project manager)	3.5
Actual effort per day	6

Table 10-5. Inventory of pages by type for each lesson.

Lesson	Type 1 Pages	Type 2 Pages	Type 3 Pages	Type 4 Pages	Assessment	Total Pages
1	2	3	1	2	1	9
2	5	1	2	2	1	11
3	3	2	3	0	1	9
4	2	1	2	3	1	9
5	4	3	1	1	1	10
6	3	2	1	1	1	8
7	3	2	2	2	1	10
8	2	3	3	1	1	10
9	1	3	2	2	1	9
10	3	1	1	3	1	9
Totals:	28	21	18	17	10	94

Table 10-6. Production effort (in hours) to create course content per lesson.

Lesson	Type 1 Pages	Type 2 Pages	Type 3 Pages	Type 4 Pages	Assessment	Total Effort
1	5.0	13.5	5.0	26.0	12.5	62.0
2	12.5	4.5	10.0	26.0	12.5	65.5
3	7.5	9.0	15.0	0.0	12.5	44.0
4	5.0	4.5	10.0	39.0	12.5	71.0
5	10.0	13.5	5.0	13.0	12.5	54.0
6	7.5	9.0	5.0	13.0	12.5	47.0
7	7.5	9.0	10.0	26.0	12.5	65.0
8	5.0	13.5	15.0	13.0	12.5	59.0
9	2.5	13.5	10.0	26.0	12.5	64.5
10	7.5	4.5	5.0	39.0	12.5	68.5
					Total effort for production:	600.5

Table 10-7. Estimated proofing and testing effort (in hours) per page.

Activity	Type 1 Pages	Type 2 Pages	Type 3 Pages	Type 4 Pages	Assessment
Script Writing	0.25	0.25	0.25	0.25	1.0
Test Case Writing	0.25	0.25	0.25	0.25	2.0
Test Execution	0.50	0.80	1.00	1.50	3.0
Total Testing Effort per Template	1.00	1.30	1.50	2.00	6.0

Table 10-8. Proofing and Testing effort (in hours) by lesson.

Lesson	Type 1 Pages	Type 2 Pages	Type 3 Pages	Type 4 Pages	Assessment	Total Effort
1	2.00	3.75	1.50	4.00	6.00	17.25
2	5.00	1.25	3.00	4.00	6.00	19.25
3	3.00	2.50	4.50	0.00	6.00	16.00
4	2.00	1.25	3.00	6.00	6.00	18.25
5	4.00	3.75	1.50	2.00	6.00	17.25
6	3.00	2.50	1.50	2.00	6.00	15.00
7	3.00	2.50	3.00	4.00	6.00	18.50
8	2.00	3.75	4.50	2.00	6.00	18.25
9	1.00	3.75	3.00	4.00	6.00	17.75
10	3.00	1.25	1.50	6.00	6.00	17.75
					Total effort for testing:	**175.25**

You may also want to create a summary table showing the combined production, proofing, and testing efforts by lesson (table 10-9).

Table 10-9. Production, proofing, and testing effort by lesson.

Lesson	Type 1 Pages	Type 2 Pages	Type 3 Pages	Type 4 Pages	Assessment	Total Effort
1	7.00	17.25	6.50	30.00	18.50	79.25
2	17.50	5.75	13.00	30.00	18.50	84.75
3	10.50	11.50	19.50	0.00	18.50	60.00
4	7.00	5.75	13.00	45.00	18.50	89.25
5	14.00	17.25	6.50	15.00	18.50	71.25
6	10.50	11.50	6.50	15.00	18.50	62.00
7	10.50	11.50	13.00	30.00	18.50	83.50
8	7.00	17.25	19.50	15.00	18.50	77.25
9	3.50	17.25	13.00	30.00	18.50	82.25
10	10.50	5.75	6.50	45.00	18.50	86.25
					Total effort for production and testing:	**775.75**

You can now summarize all activities for the project by broad category of activity as shown in table 10-10.

Table 10-10. Total estimated effort (in hours) for project.

Category	Effort (Hours)
Designing brand-new templates	31
Course content production	600
Proofing and testing	175
Focus groups	312
Administration	210
Total effort:	**1,328**

Having estimated the effort for the entire project, create a table summarizing the total number of weeks for the e-learning project, the planned number of delivery cycles, team size (in full-time equivalents, or FTEs), and a conservative estimate of an FTE's productive hours per week. Table 10-11 provides some figures for the sample e-learning project.

Table 10-11. Project management summary.

Weeks	13
Delivery Cycles	3
Team Size	3.5
Conservative estimated availability per team member (hours)	30

Time for a Reality Check

Check your estimates by dividing the total estimated effort by the number of team FTEs, divided by the number of weeks. For the sample e-learning project, the average weekly effort required per FTE is

1,328 hours ÷ 3.5 FTEs ÷ 13 weeks = 29 hours per FTE per week

This is close to your estimated team member availability. You next need to allocate the activities over the number of delivery cycles you've selected. Let's assume you've distributed effort over the three cycles as shown in table 10-12.

Table 10-12. Effort (in hours) distributed over the three delivery cycles of the project.

Activity	Delivery Cycle 1	Delivery Cycle 2	Delivery Cycle 3
Design of new templates	31	0	0
Course production	133	191	276
Proofing and testing	50	50	75
Focus groups	104	104	104
Administration	70	70	70
Weeks in cycle	4	4	5

Finally, work with your project team to create the preliminary cycle plan by carefully selecting activities for delivery cycle 1 that will allow you to demonstrate a meaningful chunk of your e-learning product at interim focus group 1. In the example, this chunk could include one entire lesson and selected pages from each of the other nine lessons to demonstrate navigation through the course. In addition, you will have complete designs for all of the brand-new templates designed for the e-learning project.

Your preliminary cycle plan would also outline your current plan for delivering the remainder of the course over delivery cycles 2 and 3.

PUBLISHING THE DELIVERY CYCLES

It is important to create the preliminary cycle plan and distribute it to the participants of the project initiation focus group, your project team, and all other stakeholders in the e-learning project within a few days after the focus group meeting. This activity in itself helps manage expectations about the remainder of the project. It builds anticipation on the part of the designated participants in the upcoming interim focus group session and galvanizes your team to develop the required deliverables in time for the session.

Table 10-13 is an example of a preliminary delivery cycle plan based on the sample e-learning project.

Table 10-13. Preliminary delivery cycle plan.

Lesson	Cycle 1	Cycle 2	Cycle 3	Total
1	72	7	0	79
2	10	61	14	85
3	55	5	0	60
4	10	69	10	89
5	10	39	22	71
6	10	12	40	62
7	10	0	74	84
8	10	0	67	77
9	10	0	72	82
10	21	56	9	86
Total effort for production:	**218**	**249**	**308**	**775**

Delivery cycle 1 yields all the lesson homepages, complete versions of lessons 1 and 3, and the exam for lesson 10. The plan leaves about 20 percent of lessons 1 and 4 for modification that might be requested in interim focus group 1. In addition, during cycle 1 the new templates identified in the project plan are prepared for use in all three cycles.

Delivery cycle 2 incorporates any requested modifications to lessons 1 and 3 coming out of interim focus group 1, completes lessons 2 and 10, and adds navigation pages to lessons 4 through 9. The plan leaves about 20 percent of lessons 4 and 9 for modification that might be requested in interim focus group 1.

Delivery cycle 3 incorporates any requested modifications to lessons 2 and 10 coming out of interim focus group 2 and completes lessons 4 through 9.

E-Learning Requirements Management

Don't be surprised if you encounter changes in requirements as you begin to produce the deliverables for cycle 1. Plan to meet informally with your e-learning customers during the crucial stages of template selection and creation of the "look" and "feel" of your e-learning product. These items need to be pinned down as quickly (and as firmly) as possible to avoid unnecessary rework during the remainder of the project. A collaborative relationship with your customer will help keep this process constructive. The delivery cycles also provide a basis for trade-offs of requirements in the remaining cycles.

However, unexpected changes in requirements may call for further discussions that need to include the project sponsor and other budget stakeholders in the project. Your risk management plan and change management plans would have spelled out how you and the customer would deal with these kinds of changes.

What Is Quality in E-Learning?

Quality remains a subjective term. Does your customer define quality in terms of appropriateness in meeting learning objectives, state-of-the-art interactivity for every page of content, stunning graphics, or ability of the product to follow complex navigation rules based on each learner's profile?

Get agreement about what constitutes quality for the product, and try to develop metrics for demonstrating your e-learning product's quality as defined by your customer. Yes, your test plans still need to make sure there are no broken page links and that your pages load on the platforms specified in the project definition; but don't lose sight of the less tangible quality measures your customer will be using, and seek to define them in ways you and your team can demonstrate.

MANAGING RISK IN E-LEARNING PROJECTS

One of your most important e-learning project management jobs during the first delivery cycle is completing the risk management tasks identified. Any activities regarding risk avoidance, risk mitigation, and contingency planning should be scheduled and completed in the early part of the cycle 1.

TRACKING PROGRESS

During the first cycle, you have the chance to conduct a "reality check" on your estimates. Your reporting for an e-learning project the size of the one in the example should be weekly. Track effort at the page level and create online forms for your team to post twice daily. If set up properly, this task takes only a minute or so but provides you with invaluable feedback to improve your ability to estimate projects.

Figure 10-2 is an example of a posting form for tracking development of pages in the lessons for the sample e-learning project.

Wherever possible, have the forms available for posting online. You can merge these report grids to derive an emerging picture of the progress your team is making toward completing the project. Consider summarizing the reports twice weekly for your team and creating a high-level report to publish weekly online for the customers, project sponsor, and stakeholders.

Always include in your reports an update of your risk management activities and a barometer of the risks that seem to be the most threatening at the current stage of your e-learning project.

Technical Reviews

During this period, plan to hold short, informal technical reviews and walk-throughs with your e-learning project team several times a week and a more formal review once a week.

Content Reviews

Your customer and SMEs serve as the sources for much of your content. In your project plan, you emphasized the criticality of getting prompt responses to content questions from your customer or their designated SME. To do so usually requires informal email or telephone contact with the customer or SME almost every day. You may also need to institute a more formal meeting on a weekly or biweekly basis.

Figure 10-2. Part of a posting form to track page development.

Date: _____   AM/PM: _____   Initials: _____

Please Post and Submit Twice Daily

Lesson 1	Text	Graphics	Navigation	Audio	Video	Total	% Complete
Page 1							
Page 2							
Page 3							
Page 4							
Page 5							
Page 6							
Page 7							
Page 8							

Lesson 2	Text	Graphics	Navigation	Audio	Video	Total	% Complete
Page 1							
Page 2							
Page 3							
Page 4							
Page 5							
Page 6							
Page 7							
Page 8							
Page 9							
Page 10							

Lesson 3	Text	Graphics	Navigation	Audio	Video	Total	% Complete
Page 1							
Page 2							
Page 3							
Page 4							
Page 5							
Page 6							

CONFIGURATION MANAGEMENT

If you have an LCMS to handle this function, great! Otherwise, work with IT to establish a central repository for e-learning content and procedures for back-up and recovery of current (and previous) versions of your e-learning content.

INTEGRATION OF E-LEARNING COMPONENTS

Your first interim focus group will demonstrate a working version of the e-learning course in its current state. Basically, you'll be demonstrating

- the main infrastructure or "shell" of the course
- shells for all of the lessons, for example, the lesson homepage and menus
- complete pages for one or more lessons.

Coordinating the efforts of multiple team members is one of the major challenges of managing your e-learning project. To keep the entire team conscious of the big picture and to allow for frequent navigation testing, you should consider creating "builds" to integrate all work completed into the ongoing working version of the e-learning course. Some organizations create builds once a week, some daily, some hourly! Normally all work should be backed up before and after the build so that it's always possible to roll back to a previous version.

Ultimately, all stakeholders will see the working version at the next interim focus group session, but you, your staff, and at least one staff member designated by the customer should be demonstrating and testing each interim version to ensure the final product is of the highest possible quality.

YOUR TURN

Well, really this entire chapter was "your turn." You had an opportunity to work your way through a project launch and project management cycles by following a sample e-learning project. If you want to try your own numbers, check out the companion Website (www.projectmanagingelearning.com) to download blank worksheets.

Consider further the issues of e-learning quality and standardization. Complete the exercises in worksheets 10-1 and 10-2. Ask others in your organization to complete the same questionnaires. Then compile the results and discuss them with your e-learning planning group.

Worksheet 10-1. Quality questionnaire.

1. When you talk about quality in e-learning for your organization, what do you mean?

2. Who should review e-learning content for courses designed for learners within the organization?

3. Should greater scrutiny be given to e-learning products designed for learners outside the walls of the organization?

4. Rank the following seven items in terms of importance in determining quality:

Rank	Item
	Content free from typographical errors
	Content free from factual errors
	Content free from offensive or potentially libelous elements
	Navigation logical and easy to follow
	System available at all times, not subject to overload
	System accessible with relative ease for learners with slower bandwidth
	Course materials available to users of all popular Web browsers

Worksheet 10-2. Standardization questionnaire.

1. To what extent is standardization of e-learning course page style valued within the organization?

2. How would standardization add to the workload of e-learning course developers within the organization?

3. How would standardization make the job of e-learning course development easier in the future?

4. Should the organization consider commissioning or purchasing templates and other standardization tools?

5. Are there creative resources within the organization that could develop templates and other standardization tools?

6. Does standardization stifle creativity?

7. Should the time and cost of developing new templates intended for reuse be charged to the current project or established as a separate charge item?

11

Rolling Out, Looking Back, Preparing for the Next Cycle

Your e-learning project is now officially under way. Furthermore, you've published a delivery schedule for the e-learning product that commits you, your team, *and the customer* to producing a real e-learning product in a series of time-boxed cycles. Each cycle culminates in a focus group convened to review the product in its evolution from a shell with only partial functionality to a fleshed-out working model of the final e-learning product and then to a final test product that comes as close as possible to meeting the ultimate needs of the customer and the e-learning audience (figure 11-1).

Among the great blessings of Web-based e-learning are its ability to keep course content current and the relative ease with which you can amend and improve design and interface elements. These blessings can sometimes look like curses when you're the project manager and face tight budgetary and time constraints. But one thing is certain: The old methods of locking in all the requirements, demanding customer sign-offs (preferably in blood), and judging the success of the project by its conformity to the original project plan are no longer viable in today's world. *The power of e-learning lies in its flexibility!*

Recognizing the inevitability of change is just the start. Your e-learning product is in many ways a living entity, and a successful one will continue to evolve even after Version 1.0 is delivered at the end of your project. However, you want to get the major architectural and high-level design decisions established as early as possible, because changes in these elements late in a project lead to wasteful rework and will often cause the project to fail altogether.

The first interim focus group session is the place where you bring together the project team, stakeholders, and a representative sampling of the e-learning audience to examine the overall structure and design of the product. Participants will see real working versions of some of its learning modules, and either approve the current general direction for the product or give redirection

Figure 11-1. The evolution of an e-learning project.

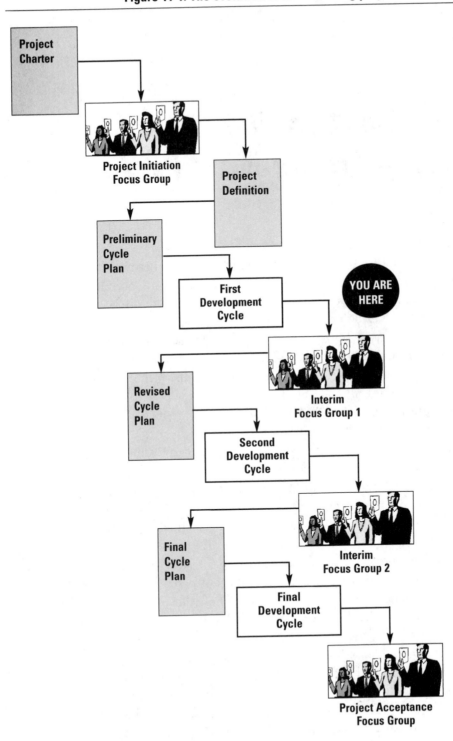

to you and your team. Remember, the e-learning project has been a collaborative effort, and there should be relatively few surprises. But, if you've overlooked something or if market changes or other considerations mandate a new direction, you need to address such changes right away.

BALANCING ORDER AND CHAOS

Focus groups and time-boxed delivery cycles allow you to structure your project, keep it accountable, and establish fixed points where the e-learning product will come under the careful scrutiny of your customer and stakeholders well in advance of final delivery. This approach provides flexibility without anarchy. The emphasis on delivering a working product ensures that you and your team will concentrate on what your customer cares about most.

At the same time, as a project manager, you realize the importance of documentation, planning, and progress reporting to ensure that the final e-learning product arrives with all the necessary supporting materials and that it meets all necessary infrastructure requirements. You must also be sure that all parties involved in the ultimate deployment of the product are aware of its progress toward completion and its status with respect to cost, features, and delivery timetables. How can you keep track of it all?

THE PROJECT MANAGER'S TOOLKIT

Your earlier work during the project definition stage produced two important documents (context diagrams) to manage the overall scope of the product as well as the scope of the process used to generate the product (chapter 3). This is also where your priority matrix, progress communication plan, risk management plan, testing strategies, and change management plan come into play. Let's see how these tools will help you steer your project to a successful completion.

Scope Management

Believe it or not, context diagrams are a valuable, straightforward way of keeping your project from becoming a victim of scope creep. These diagrams, though quite high level, provided everyone involved in the project with models showing

■ who and what were to interact with the project in creating the product
■ who and what would interact with the product once it was delivered.

Each arrow on the diagram for your e-learning product represented a flow of information or content. No one should be surprised if information or content details change during the execution of your e-learning project. What should set off alarms would be new arrows or new boxes on the diagrams. These diagram elements indicate the introduction of new individuals or systems or the discovery of whole new categories of information or content to be handled by your e-learning product.

Any time it's necessary to redraw either of the diagrams, it's probably also time to reexamine the project budget and timeline. Is the change disruptive to the current project delivery schedule? Are more resources required? Do reports have to be prepared for a new audience?

Naturally, the most important question must be: Is the change in scope absolutely necessary? If the change is the result of a new government regulation or reporting requirement, then the answer is affirmative. This is also true if the business needs of your organization suddenly mandate delivering a whole new type of content or delivering content over a new medium. For example, if the salesforce requires e-learning course delivery over PDAs instead of at their desktop computers, then you would likely have to rescope the project.

The Priority Matrix Revisited

As your project progresses, the customer's original priorities may change. You captured those original priorities with a simple but powerful tool called the priority matrix (chapter 3). At the beginning of the project, cost may have been the top priority to the customer, with time being a close second. That means that quality/scope would be dependent on the time and money limitations placed on the project. By the time you reach the first interim focus group session, the customer has identified several new features that seem essential to the success of the e-learning product.

The priority matrix allows you to ask the customer: Is quality/scope now the top priority? If so, it will be necessary to reprioritize the other two elements in the matrix. Because quality/scope is now the highest priority, should the second priority be cost or schedule? If cost is the second priority, then it *may* be possible to deliver the project with the new features within budget if it is feasible to extend the time available to complete the project. (Note that the extended time very likely will add some cost, however.) If time is the second priority, then you may be able to deliver the project with the new features on time if you have additional funds for staffing, consultants, and so forth. Once again, make sure you publish the revised priority matrix to keep everyone informed whenever there is a change in priority.

Progress Communication—Just Enough, Just in Time

The information you gather about your team's e-learning project progress should be detailed enough to keep you aware of the project's status at all times. The information you communicate to the project sponsor, the customer, and the project stakeholders should be concise and should concentrate on the information they care most about (oftentimes budget and what they're going to see at the next focus group session). You also need to keep visible the most threatening risks to your project, along with what has been agreed upon with respect to your response to a risk if it does occur.

Plan to publish your progress reports on the second business day of each week. This way, you can gather data through the end of the following week and have a full day to analyze and summarize the previous week's activities to produce a simple, meaningful report.

Have your team members email you their weekly status reports by late Friday afternoon. Figure 11-2 is a rendering of a sample report form used by an e-learning project team.

Figure 11-2. Sample report form.*

Weekly Status Report for Project Team Member

\<Your Name\>

For Week Ending: \<Date\>

Planned accomplishments:
-
-

Unplanned accomplishments:
-
-

Planned but not completed:
-
-

Planned for next week:
-
-

Goals for this week:
-
-

Work schedule this week: \<Dates\>

Monday	Tuesday	Wednesday	Thursday	Friday

Planned work schedule next week: \<Dates\>

Monday	Tuesday	Wednesday	Thursday	Friday

*Form may be downloaded from www.projectmanagingelearning.com.

Proofing and Testing

Testing and proofing should be ongoing throughout the project. Develop some standard forms for keeping track of testing and proofing processes. Figure 11-3 is a very simple but very practical example of such a form.

Focus Group Sessions and Change Management

Each interim focus group session will result in a number of decisions and refinements for the final e-learning product. Sessions can be as short as a couple of hours or run up to a full day in length. For most e-learning projects, though, a half-day session should be adequate.

As with the other forms used to manage your project, simplicity should rule over complexity. Use a simple form to capture the main elements, and have your session scribe document more details as needed and publish them as addenda to the main report form. Figure 11-4 is another sample form.

Publishing the Revised Delivery Plan

Immediately after the first interim focus group session, you and your team can determine any required changes to completed modules and schedule the delivery of additional content for the next scheduled interim focus group session. Table 11-1 shows the revised delivery cycle plan resulting from an interim focus group session. Compare these figures with the preliminary cycle plan shown in table 11-2.

Lesson 1 took 5 hours more than planned. However, the focus group requested only a couple of minor changes. Therefore, the total projected effort for lesson 1 will be 57 hours, only 2 of which will occur in cycle 2. Lesson 3 took less time than estimated, but the focus group requested several changes that will add to the overall effort required to complete the project. The other lessons varied only slightly from the original plan.

For cycle 2, lessons 1 and 3 will be revised as requested, lessons 2 and 10 will be prepared for final review, and the assessment pages for the remaining lessons will be put into place.

The Last Interim Focus Group and the Final Cycle Plan

Let's now look at what might happen in the last of your interim focus group sessions. You and your team completed lesson 3 according to the focus group's original specifications, but now the focus group has presented additional requirements based on a change in a procedure. This change means that lesson 3 will require 15 hours more effort in the third delivery cycle. So, now, the final delivery cycle plan looks like table 11-3.

The final delivery cycle plan calls for 53 hours more development work than originally planned.

Figure 11-3. Form for tracking and proofing processes.*

Course Title:
Date Reviewed:
Version Number:
Reviewed By:

Chapter 1

Page #	Audio	Text	Media Image	PDF	Exercise

Chapter 2

Page #	Audio	Text	Media Image	PDF	Exercise

Chapter 3

Page #	Audio	Text	Media Image	PDF	Exercise

Chapter 4

Page #	Audio	Text	Media Image	PDF	Exercise

Chapter 5

Page #	Audio	Text	Media Image	PDF	Exercise

*Form may be downloaded from www.projectmanagingelearning.com.

Figure 11-4. Sample form to document focus group results.*

Project Name _____
Client Name _____

Project Name _____
Client Name _____

Agenda Topics
- Project Updates
- Previews—Demonstration
- Navigation
- Sub-Navigation Sample
- Next Steps
- Strategy—Long-Range Planning

Project Updates
- Sample Text
  - Sample: Insert meeting minutes within the project meeting notes using a color code to highlight your notes

Previews—Demonstration
- Sample Text—insert images when applicable
  - Sample text: Insert meeting minutes within the project meeting notes using a color code to highlight your notes

Tab Navigation
- Sample Text—insert images when applicable
  - Sample text: Insert meeting minutes within the project meeting notes using a color code to highlight your notes

Sub-Navigation Sample
- Sample Text—insert images when applicable
  - Sample text: Insert meeting minutes within the project meeting notes using a color code to highlight your notes

Next Steps
- Sample text
  - Sample text: Insert meeting minutes within the project meeting notes using a color code to highlight your notes

Strategy—Long-Range Planning
- Sample text: Insert meeting minutes within the project meeting notes using a color code to highlight your notes

Action Items
Overall Project Items

Color Coded Names	Sample Text Tasks

Site or Module Changes

Color Coded Names	Sample Text Tasks

Navigation

System Tasks

Misc.

*Form may be downloaded from www.projectmanagingelearning.com.

Table 11-1. Revised delivery cycle plan.

Lesson	Cycle 1*	Cycle 2	Cycle 3	Total
1	55	2	0	57
2	20	40	5	65
3	29	20	0	49
4	14	14	43	71
5	21	14	19	54
6	4	14	29	47
7	5	14	47	66
8	3	14	42	59
9	5	14	46	65
10	18	45	6	69
Total effort for production:	**174**	**191**	**237**	**602**

*Actual

Table 11-2. Preliminary delivery cycle plan.

Lesson	Cycle 1	Cycle 2	Cycle 3	Total
1	50	12	0	62
2	17	48	0	65
3	35	9	0	44
4	17	13	42	72
5	17	13	25	55
6	5	13	30	48
7	5	13	48	66
8	5	13	42	60
9	5	13	48	66
10	17	45	7	69
Total effort for production:	**173**	**192**	**242**	**607**

Table 11-3. Final delivery cycle plan.

Lesson	Cycle 1*	Cycle 2*	Cycle 3	Total
1	55	5	0	60
2	20	50	7	77
3	29	20	15	64
4	14	14	43	71
5	21	14	19	54
6	3	14	29	46
7	5	14	47	66
8	3	14	42	59
9	5	14	46	65
10	18	45	35	98
Total effort for production:	**173**	**204**	**283**	**660**

*Actual   *Actual

Risk Management and Change Management Revisited

This example illustrates how you, as an e-learning project manager, can apply risk management and change management, in addition to a well-orchestrated communication plan, to manage expectations and prepare your customer and project sponsor for handling unexpected changes in project requirements. Here are the areas where an e-learning project manager should have laid groundwork before the "surprise changes" that occurred in the last interim focus group:

- *Risk management:* Let's face it: Requirement changes will always be risks for e-learning projects. In the example given, your risk management plan should have addressed what would happen if there were last-minute changes in requirements.
- *Change management:* Your change management plan should have spelled out how allocations of additional funds or extensions of time would be approved to cover additional effort required because of a change in the project deliverables.
- *Communication plan:* Your weekly reports should have been listing the most threatening risks for your e-learning project and would have included a statement about the likelihood of requirement changes. Keeping such statements visible to all those involved in your e-learning project gives them adequate time to keep you informed if they see changes looming on the horizon.
- *The priority matrix:* Continue to keep the relative priorities of time, cost, and quality/scope visible to everyone involved in the project. A last-minute change in requirements, if deemed essential to the project, may require the sponsor and customer to reprioritize time and cost to obtain the required change. The revision of the matrix is not just a formality; it is official recognition of a decision made.

If you have used all four of these important project management tools, you will have a much easier time of negotiating additional time or resources to complete the project. Your customer and project sponsor may also be better prepared to accept compromise measures, such as cutting back on scope or reducing the testing effort, which may diminish the quality or scope of the e-learning product but avoid increased costs or delayed delivery.

How well you've communicated these trade-offs up to the time of the change in requirements will help determine how readily you can successfully manage such a change. This is where e-learning project management borders of becoming an art. But, the science of e-learning project management requires the use of the basic tools of risk and change management, a solid communication plan, and strict observance of your progress reporting obligations. If you've used these tools, the art part is easy!

YOUR TURN

Which of the tools suggested here do you intend to use for your e-learning projects? Which ones will be unique for every project? Can you use any of the suggested tools as-is, or will you need to adapt them? Can you make these available on the Web? Use worksheet 11-1, and add any other tools you've heard about to the list. You may, of course, download the worksheet from www.projectmanagingelearning.com.

Worksheet 11-1. Project management tools presented here.

Tool or Technique	Unique for Each Project?	Use As-Is or Adapt?	If Adapt, Estimated Effort to Adapt and Due Date
Project context diagram	Yes / No	As-Is / Adapt	
Product context diagram	Yes / No	As-Is / Adapt	
Priority matrix	Yes / No	As-Is / Adapt	
Risk assessment lists	Yes / No	As-Is / Adapt	
Estimating grids	Yes / No	As-Is / Adapt	
Template definition grids	Yes / No	As-Is / Adapt	
Cycle planning worksheets	Yes / No	As-Is / Adapt	
Weekly status report forms	Yes / No	As-Is / Adapt	
Testing and proofing forms	Yes / No	As-Is / Adapt	
Focus group session notes	Yes / No	As-Is / Adapt	
Sources other than this book (use rows below)	Yes / No	As-Is / Adapt	
	Yes / No	As-Is / Adapt	
	Yes / No	As-Is / Adapt	
	Yes / No	As-Is / Adapt	
	Yes / No	As-Is / Adapt	

Consider this scenario: Your current project is already under way to create a sales staff training course to provide new sales staff with basic product and sales techniques for your company.

You originally created an e-learning product context diagram (worksheet 11-2) to illustrate how the course was going to work. However, at the first interim focus group session, the sales managers indicated that they would like the following changes:

1. Allow sales managers online access to staff participation statistics, monitor staff progress through the course, and correlate course participation with staff performance figures from the sales database.
2. Provide usage statistics to the HR department.
3. Provide ad hoc product and procedure information to staff via their PDAs over wireless connections.
4. Instead of having the course development group update content online, the sales managers now would like a user-friendly tool to allow them to make their own changes to the course directly online.

Now, redraw the product context diagram on worksheet 11-2 to reflect their proposed requirements, and decide which changes will have the greatest impact on the time and resources needed to complete the project.

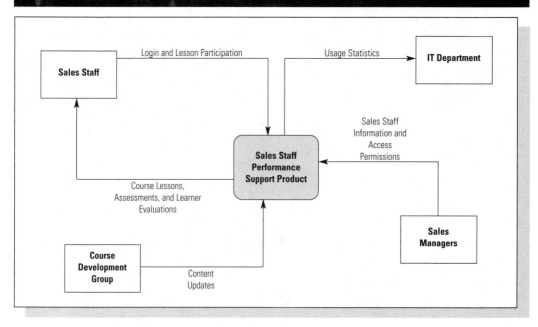

Worksheet 11-2. Product context diagram.

12

Looking Ahead: Building on E-Learning Successes and Lessons Learned

Your first e-learning project is now coming to an end. It's almost certain that many things about the project—and about the originally planned e-learning product itself—did not turn out quite the way that you, your team, your project sponsor, or your customer originally envisioned. Many of these variances were inevitable and desirable. The goal was to produce the right e-learning product—not necessarily the one specified at project definition!

It is likely though that there were some surprises that maybe shouldn't have been *quite* so unexpected and that you and your team can better anticipate in the future. To continue developing a solid e-learning project management initiative within your organization, you need to dedicate time and thought to evaluation of every e-learning project and learn from your successes and mistakes. Capturing and sharing this project management knowledge is one of the most important components of good project management.

DELIVERING THE PRODUCT, BUILDING MOMENTUM

The project acceptancce focus group is the occasion both to demonstrate the final product and to prepare for the continuation of your organization's e-learning initiative. The first consideration must be whether the e-learning product meets the customer's needs. The final delivery cycle should involve even closer collaboration with the customer so that the project acceptancce focus group serves as the ultimate validation of the product. In addition, the participants should receive a review form to complete and submit at the end of the session. Figure 12-1 provides a sample of such a review form.

Each member of the project team should complete a similar, but more detailed form, such as the one in figure 12-2.

Figure 12-1. Review form for the final focus group.*

Focus Group Participant E-Learning Project Evaluation Review Form

Project: **Review Date:**

Your Name:

Your Department:

Your Role in Project:

E-LEARNING PRODUCT EVALUATION

What is your overall assessment of the e-learning product based on your participation in the project and in the product demonstrations presented in the Focus Groups?

What do you especially like about this product?

What do you find less than satisfactory about this product?

What could make this a better product?

How long a shelf life do you predict for this product?

EVALUATION OF THE PRODUCT DELIVERY PROCESS

What is your overall assessment of the process used to create this e-learning product?

Did participation in the Focus Groups provide sufficient visibility of the project's progress?

What, if anything, was especially helpful about these sessions?

What, if anything, should be omitted from these sessions?

How could the Focus Group process improve?

How useful were the Weekly Progress Reports in keeping you informed about the progress of the project team in completing the e-learning product?

What, if anything, was especially helpful about these reports?

What, if anything, should be omitted from these reports?

How could these reports be improved?

*May be downloaded from www.projectmanagingelearning.com.

Figure 12-1. Review form for the final focus group (continued).*

RISK MANAGEMENT/CHANGE MANAGEMENT
Throughout the project, you were alerted to problems that potentially could come up to threaten the project. Did any of these actually occur? If so, do prior warnings help prepare you and those involved in the project to deal with them more effectively?
What unexpected problems, if any, came up to threaten the project and the successful delivery of the project? Are any of these likely to come up again in similar e-learning projects in the future?
How effectively did the project handle these threats?
How effectively did the project deal with mandatory changes in requirements or changes in priorities during the delivery of the e-learning product?
RECOMMENDATION FOR THE FUTURE
How do you view the current e-learning product as part of your organization's overall e-learning effort?
What would you consider the "next step" for your organization?
Use this space for any other comments you'd like to provide:

*May be downloaded from www.projectmanagingelearning.com.

THE FINAL REPORT

Within 10 days of the final focus group session, you and your team should meet, analyze the responses to the review forms, and prepare a final report for publication. The following sections outline the issues to be covered in the final report.

Evaluating the Product: Level 0 Evaluation

Based on the evaluations by all participants, indicate how successful you and your team were in delivering the e-learning product the customer and stakeholders requested. How many of the requested features actually were incorporated into the final product? Were there new technical or design elements introduced into

Figure 12-2. Review form for project team members.*

Project Team Member E-Learning Project Evaluation Review Form

Project: **Review Date:**

Your Name:

Your Department:

Your Role in Project:

E-LEARNING PRODUCT EVALUATION

What is your overall assessment of the success of the e-learning product?

What part of the e-learning product did you take an active part in developing?

How close do you think the product comes to meeting the customer's expectations?

Where does it fall short?

What changes are likely to be required in the future?

EVALUATION OF THE PRODUCT DELIVERY PROCESS

What is your overall assessment of the process used to create this e-learning product?

Were the Focus Groups helpful in getting the product delivered to the customer?

What, if anything, was especially helpful about these sessions?

What, if anything, about these sessions would you consider a waste of time?

How could the Focus Group process improve?

Do you think preparing and distributing Weekly Progress Reports was helpful?

What, if anything, was especially helpful about these reports?

What, if anything, should be omitted from these reports?

How could these reports be improved?

*May be downloaded from www.projectmanagingelearning.com.

Figure 12-2. Review form for project team members (continued).*

RISK MANAGEMENT/CHANGE MANAGEMENT

Did taking time to identify and communicate risks to the project actually help prepare the team and the customer for dealing with problems that occurred?

What unexpected problems, if any, came up to threaten the project and the successful delivery of the project? Are any of these likely to come up again in similar e-learning projects in the future?

How effectively did you and the team handle these threats?

How well were you and the team able to respond to changes in requirements? How much rework was required?

RECOMMENDATION FOR THE FUTURE

If you were to select the next major e-learning project for your organization, what would you recommend?

What tools did you develop for this project that you can use in subsequent projects?

Use this space for any other comments you'd like to provide:

*May be downloaded from www.projectmanagingelearning.com.

the product? How will your organization carry out level 4 evaluation of the product once it goes into production (Horton, 2001b)?

Evaluating the Process

Using the evaluations of all participants and your discussions with the team, the customer, and project sponsor, determine how successfully you and your team were in collaboration with the customer to produce the e-learning product. Address the following issues:

- *How accurate were your estimates?* Consider both estimated effort and actual effort for tasks that did not change and areas where an expanded requirement demanded greater effort than originally estimated. The first category of variance indicates the need to reevaluate your estimates for such tasks. The second category of variance is the result of a change of requirements and doesn't necessarily mean your estimating skills need to improve.
- *Was your approach too heavy or too light?* Were there too many focus group sessions, just the right number, or would more sessions have resulted in

a better product? Did the sessions run too long? Were the progress reports you and the team produced "overkill" for the project, or do you need to provide greater detail in the reports? Striking the right balance in your e-learning projects is crucial for a successful e-learning initiative. Don't be afraid to make adjustments if you sense you are over- or under-communicating during the course of your project. Use the experience gained from the current project to help decide how many focus group sessions you need and the level of detail your reports should have.

■ *What technological discoveries did you make that will benefit future projects?* Did you introduce any new productivity tools? Should future teams consider acquiring new tools? To ensure continued success and continuity for projects, should each project dedicate a certain percentage of effort to overall process improvement (for example, incorporation of new tools, preparation for migration to new infrastructures)?

■ *How well did the overall collaborative process work?* Were there adequate opportunities to communicate with the customer, e-learning project sponsor, and SMEs? Were key individuals readily available to make decisions between focus group sessions? How well did the team and the customer balance flexibility and focus on schedule and budget constraints?

Past "Gotcha's" and Future Risks

Take time to review the risk management activities used for your e-learning project and see how well you anticipated problems before they occurred. Did you spend undue amounts of time preparing for contingencies that never came about? Even more important, were there any surprises that you had not addressed in your risk management plan? Are any of these likely to occur again in subsequent e-learning projects? If so, how can you anticipate them for the next e-learning project's risk management plan?

Continuous Needs Assessment

In completing the current e-learning project, did the customer, the project sponsor, or your team members identify unmet requirements or future needs that subsequent projects should address? If you are part of a large organization, it probably has a comprehensive e-learning strategy into which these newly identified elements could fit. If you are the person in charge of e-learning for the entire organization, you can use this new information to help identify what's next for your e-learning initiative.

How Can You Do Better?

Hindsight really is always best. You, your team, and virtually all involved in completing the current project have probably identified many ways that could have made this project work better. The bad news in the past has been that no one ever formally puts this learning into practice. The good news is that e-learning is here to stay and that whatever you have learned about this project will more than likely apply to your next e-learning project if you take time to reflect on what you can do differently next time and incorporate those insights into the next project plan.

Creating Templates for E-Learning Components

How many new designs, procedures, report forms, and so forth can become part of your ongoing e-learning project manager's toolkit? Make every effort to standardize and reuse project and content artifacts to maximize your organization's effectiveness and provide better tools for subsequent e-learning projects and products.

WHERE IS THE NEXT FRONTIER?

E-learning is still in its infancy. You don't want to slash your organization with a great deal of bleeding-edge technology, but you do want to stay aware of what is waiting on the horizon and lay as much groundwork as possible for future innovation. Spend time looking at new tools and techniques, attending e-learning conferences, reading e-learning publications, and brainstorming with your team, your organization's planners, and your colleagues to continually find new and better ways of implementing e-learning.

CONCLUSION

Every minute devoted to the kind of project evaluation described here is an investment in your organization's e-learning effort. Continuous needs assessment—along with continuous improvement of the delivery process—will help ensure your organization's success in the world of e-learning.

YOUR TURN

Ask others in your organization who are involved in e-learning projects to complete either the focus group participant version (worksheet 12-1) or the project team member version (worksheet 12-2) of the review form depending on their roles in the last project they participated in. You, too, should complete the project team member e-learning review form for the last project (e-learning or otherwise) you were involved in. You may download copies of the forms from the companion Website (www.projectmanaging.elearning.com), if you wish.

Worksheet 12-1. Review form for your final focus group.*

Focus Group Participant E-Learning Project Evaluation Review Form

Project: **Review Date:**

Your Name:

Your Department:

Your Role in Project:

E-LEARNING PRODUCT EVALUATION

What is your overall assessment of the e-learning product based on your participation in the project and in the product demonstrations presented in the Focus Groups?

What do you especially like about this product?

What do you find less than satisfactory about this product?

What could make this a better product?

How long a shelf life do you predict for this product?

EVALUATION OF THE PRODUCT DELIVERY PROCESS

What is your overall assessment of the process used to create this e-learning product?

Did participation in the Focus Groups provide sufficient visibility of the project's progress?

What, if anything, was especially helpful about these sessions?

What, if anything, should be omitted from these sessions?

How could the Focus Group process improve?

How useful were the Weekly Progress Reports in keeping you informed about the progress of the project team in completing the e-learning product?

What, if anything, was especially helpful about these reports?

What, if anything, should be omitted from these reports?

How could these reports be improved?

*May be downloaded from www.projectmanagingelearning.com.

Worksheet 12-1. Review form for your final focus group (continued).*

RISK MANAGEMENT/CHANGE MANAGEMENT

Throughout the project, you were alerted to problems that potentially could come up to threaten the project. Did any of these actually occur? If so, do prior warnings help prepare you and those involved in the project to deal with them more effectively?

What unexpected problems, if any, came up to threaten the project and the successful delivery of the project? Are any of these likely to come up again in similar e-learning projects in the future?

How effectively did the project handle these threats?

How effectively did the project deal with mandatory changes in requirements or changes in priorities during the delivery of the e-learning product?

RECOMMENDATION FOR THE FUTURE

How do you view the current e-learning product as part of your organization's overall e-learning effort?

What would you consider the "next step" for your organization?

Use this space for any other comments you'd like to provide:

*May be downloaded from www.projectmanagingelearning.com.

Arrange to meet with everyone who completed a form and briefly exchange overviews of prior project experiences and a few highlights from the evaluation form. Use worksheet 12-3 to brainstorm "do's," "don'ts," and "gotcha's" about e-learning project management based on the group's sharing. Refine the list and consider incorporating it as part of your ongoing e-learning project management best practices effort.

Worksheet 12-2. Review form for project team members.*

Project Team Member E-Learning Project Evaluation Review Form

Project: **Review Date:**

Your Name:

Your Department:

Your Role in Project:

E-LEARNING PRODUCT EVALUATION

What is your overall assessment of the success of the e-learning product?

What part of the e-learning product did you take an active part in developing?

How close do you think the product comes to meeting the customer's expectations?

Where does it fall short?

What changes are likely to be required in the future?

EVALUATION OF THE PRODUCT DELIVERY PROCESS

What is your overall assessment of the process used to create this e-learning product?

Were the Focus Groups helpful in getting the product delivered to the customer?

What, if anything, was especially helpful about these sessions?

What, if anything, about these sessions would you consider a waste of time?

How could the Focus Group process improve?

Do you think preparing and distributing Weekly Progress Reports was helpful?

What, if anything, was especially helpful about these reports?

What, if anything, should be omitted from these reports?

How could these reports be improved?

*May be downloaded from www.projectmanagingelearning.com.

Worksheet 12-2. Review form for project team members (continued).*

RISK MANAGEMENT/CHANGE MANAGEMENT

Did taking time to identify and communicate risks to the project actually help prepare the team and the customer for dealing with problems that occurred?

What unexpected problems, if any, came up to threaten the project and the successful delivery of the project? Are any of these likely to come up again in similar e-learning projects in the future?

How effectively did you and the team handle these threats?

How well were you and the team able to respond to changes in requirements? How much rework was required?

RECOMMENDATION FOR THE FUTURE

If you were to select the next major e-learning project for your organization, what would you recommend?

What tools did you develop for this project that you can use in subsequent projects?

Use this space for any other comments you'd like to provide:

*May be downloaded from www.projectmanagingelearning.com.

Worksheet 12-3. E-Learning project management "do's," "don'ts," and "gotcha's."

E-Learning Project "Do's": Things That Work and Should Become Standard Practice

E-Learning Project "Don'ts": Things That Didn't Work and Should Be Avoided on Future E-Learning Projects

E-Learning Project "Gotcha's": These Things Happen to Your Project, so LOOK OUT!

References

The American Heritage Dictionary of the English Language (4th edition). (2000). Boston: Houghton Mifflin Company.

Horton, W. (2001a). *Leading E-Learning.* Alexandria, VA: ASTD.

Horton, W. (2001b). *Evaluating E-Learning.* Alexandria, VA: ASTD.

Russell, L. (2000). *Project Management for Trainers: Stop "Winging It" and Get Control of Your Training Projects.* Alexandria, VA: ASTD.

Additional Resources

Beck, K. (2000). *Extreme Programming Explained: Embrace Change.* Boston: Addison-Wesley.

Beck, K., and M. Fowler. (2001). *Planning Extreme Programming.* Boston: Addison-Wesley.

Brooks, F.P., Jr. (1995). *The Mythical Man-Month: Essays on Software Engineering.* Reading, MA: Addison-Wesley.

Cockburn, A. (2001). *Agile Software Development.* Boston: Addison-Wesley.

DeMarco, T., and T. Lister. (1999). *Peopleware: Productive Projects and Teams.* New York: Dorset House Publishing.

Downes, L., C. Mui, and N. Negroponte. (2000). *Unleashing the Killer App: Digital Strategies for Market Dominance* (Revised edition). Boston: Harvard Business School Press.

Dyché, J. (2001). *The CRM Handbook.* Boston: Addison-Wesley.

Hall, B. (1997). *Web-Based Training Cookbook.* New York: John Wiley & Sons.

Harvard Business Review. (1998). *Harvard Business Review on Knowledge Management.* Boston: Harvard Business School Press.

Highsmith, J.A., III. (1999). *Adaptive Software Development: A Collaborative Approach to Managing Complex Systems.* New York: Dorset House Publishing.

Horton, W. (2000). *Designing Web-Based Training: How to Teach Anyone Anything Anywhere Anytime.* New York: John Wiley & Sons.

Jeffries, R., A. Anderson, and C. Hendrickson. (2000). *Extreme Programming Installed.* Boston: Addison-Wesley.

Kerzner, H. (2000). *Project Management: A Systems Approach to Planning, Scheduling, and Controlling* (7th edition). New York: John Wiley & Sons.

Lewis, J.P. (2001). *Fundamentals of Project Management (Worksmart Series).* New York: AMACOM Books.

McConnell, S. (1996). *Rapid Development: Taming Wild Software Schedules.* Redmond, WA: Microsoft Press.

McConnell, S. (1998). *Software Project Survival Guide: How to Be Sure Your First Important Project Isn't Your Last.* Redmond, WA: Microsoft Press.

Poppendieck, M. (2001, February). "Keeping the Customer Involved: Three Steps to Success." *Best Practices in IT Leadership, 2*(2), 6–7.

Project Management Institute Standards Committee. (2000). *A Guide to the Project Management Body of Knowledge.* Newtown Square, PA: PMI Publishing Division.

Rosenberg, M.J. (2001). *E-Learning: Strategies for Delivering Knowledge in the Digital Age.* New York: McGraw-Hill.

Russell, L. (1999). *The Accelerated Learning Fieldbook: Making the Instructional Process Fast, Flexible, and Fun.* San Francisco: Jossey-Bass.

Schank, R. (1997). *Virtual Learning.* New York: McGraw-Hill.

Schrage, M. (1990). *Shared Minds: The New Technologies of Collaboration.* New York: Random House.

Shackelford, W. (2001, January). "Shifting IT from Process to Product: Methodologies for the New Millennium." *Best Practices in IT Leadership, 2*(1), 1.

Shackelford, W. (2001, November). "The Art of Smart: Cultivating Customer Loyalty Through E-Learning." *Cutter IT Journal, 14*(11), 34–39.

Verzuh, E. (1999). *The Fast Forward MBA in Project Management.* New York: John Wiley & Sons.

Wood, J., and D. Silver. (1995). *Joint Application Development.* New York: John Wiley & Sons.

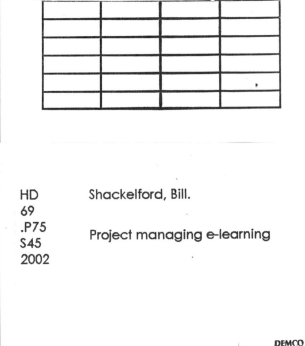

About the Author

Bill Shackelford came to the field of e-learning via an unlikely path. He received his bachelor's degree of arts in Germanic languages and literature and a master's degree of music from Indiana University. He has pursued additional studies at Indiana University, University of Hamburg, Illinois Institute of Technology, and the University of Illinois in higher education administration, German, musicology, business administration, and computer science.

Working in the 1970s in college admissions and financial aid, he served as a trainer for the U.S. Office of Education and on numerous state, regional, and national committees. In the late 1970s, he moved to the area of IT management and training at the University of Illinois's Chicago campus. In 1982, he founded Shackelford & Associates, an organization that specializes in systems design and training.

With more than 30 years' experience in education and training, Bill served as president of CODE, one of Chicago's two major IT training professional organizations and has been a featured presenter at numerous e-learning conferences and workshops in the United States and abroad. In addition, Bill is an authority on IT project management, presenting workshops and seminars throughout North America. Bill served as editor of *Best Practices in IT Leadership,* and has recently been selected to serve as guest editor for *Cutter IT Journal.* He also teaches online in the Keller Graduate School of Management's master's degree of business administration program and is collaborating on a book about e-learning standards. He is also contributing to a new book on Extreme Programming games and simulations. His article on e-learning and customer relationship management appeared in the *Cutter IT Journal* and was selected for inclusion in Cutter's *A Practical Guide to Customer Relationship Management.* His article on ADL/SCORM is scheduled for publication in *T + D* in late 2002.

He still keeps up with his musical pursuits as an internationally recognized opera critic, editor of the *Wagner News* for the Wagner Society of America, and the Chicago correspondent for *Opera* magazine. Bill has recently taken up golf and is testing the loyalty of his more accomplished friends and colleagues. He may be reached through his Website: www.projectmanagingelearning.com.